FORM…
OF THE HEART

The WHY and HOW of being a Catholic today

RAYMOND FRIEL

redemptorist
publications

Published by **Redemptorist Publications**
Wol's Lane, Chawton, Hampshire, GU34 3HQ, UK
Tel. +44 (0)1420 88222, Fax. +44 (0)1420 88805
Email rp@rpbooks.co.uk, www.rpbooks.co.uk

A registered charity limited by guarantee
Registered in England 03261721

First Published February 2022

Edited by Barbara Spender
Designed by Emma Repetti

ISBN 9780852316054

A CIP catalogue record for this book is available from the British Library.

Imprimatur: + Declan Lang
Bishop of Clifton
December 2021

Imprimatur is a declaration that a book or pamphlet is considered to be free from doctrinal or moral error. It is not implied that those who have granted the Imprimatur agree with the contents.

The publisher gratefully acknowledges permission to use the following copyright material: Excerpts from the New Revised Standard Version of the Bible: Anglicised Edition, © 1989, 1995, Division of Christian Education of the National Council of the Churches of Christ in the United States of America. Used by permission. All rights reserved.

Printed and bound by John Dollin, Printing Sevices Ltd.,
Whitchurch, Hants., RG28 7BB

Acknowledgements

There are a number of people I'd like to thank for their support with this book. A small group of friends were kind enough to help either with formative conversations, or by reading and commenting on draft versions of the manuscript: James Alison, Clive Chapman, Peter Fleetwood, Karen Foong, Maurice Glasman, Damian Howard, Eamonn Mulcahy, Jenny Sinclair, Euan Tait and David Wells. My sincere thanks to them. Thanks also to Barbara Spender, my patient and skilful editor, and to the wonderful team at Redemptorist. Thanks as ever to my wife Janet for her love and friendship over the years and through the ups and downs of my projects; and to our dog, Mabel, for many hours of silent companionship while I wrestled with the things of heaven and earth.

By the same author

Seeing the River (Edinburgh: Polygon, 1995)

Southfields Vol 1-6, ed. with Richard Price (London: Southfields Press, 1995-2000)

Renfrewshire in Old Photographs, with Richard Price (Glasgow: Mariscat, 2000)

PS Nos 1-7, ed. with Richard Price (London: published by Richard Price, 2006-2012)

Stations of the Heart (Cambridge: Salt, 2008)

How to Survive Working in a Catholic School, with Sister Judith Russi (Chawton: Redemptorist Publications, 2013)

How to Survive in Leadership in a Catholic School (Chawton: Redemptorist Publications, 2015)

The Revolution of Tenderness: Being a Catholic in Today's Church (Chawton: Redemptorist Publications, 2016)

Gospel Values for Catholic Schools: a practical guide for today (Chawton: Redemptorist Publications, 2017)

Prayers for Schools: original prayers and resources for teachers and chaplains (Chawton: Redemptorist Publications, 2018)

At Your Side: a book for those who pray, those who want to pray and those who lead prayer, with David Wells (Chawton: Redemptorist Publications, 2020)

Dedication

In memory of my parents

Francis Gabriel Friel (1930-2010)

and Ellen Friel (1933-2019)

my first teachers in the faith

"For where your treasure is,

there your heart will be also."

Matthew 6:21

"The mind seeks to understand the why and how

of the Christian life, in order to adhere and

respond to what the Lord is asking."

Catechism of the Catholic Church, 2705

CONTENTS

Introduction

It might be better to start by saying what this book is not. It's not a book for those interested in becoming a Catholic (although it might help on that journey). It's not an A-Z of Catholic belief. It's more of an introduction, or perhaps re-introduction, to what I consider to be the basics of being a Catholic, the why and how. People in other Christian denominations will, I hope, also get something out of this book. We have a lot in common.

The book is aimed primarily at a lot of people I know in the Church, whose formation in the faith may have stopped around the age of fourteen, roughly the time they were confirmed. This book is for anyone who is a baptised member of the Church who'd like to pick up where they left off all those years ago. The people I have in mind may well go to Mass, or maybe not. They may not read much sacred scripture, they may have some notion of what prayer is but don't practise it all that often. They want to live a good life but are sometimes confused about what that looks like.

This book won't answer all the questions about how to live in this world as a Catholic disciple of Jesus Christ, but will, I hope, offer some guiding principles, not least the why and the how. To cut to the end (spoiler alert!), the why of our faith is that God loves us and wants us to flourish in a new creation. The great pattern of Christian faith is God's gift followed by our gratitude, proclamation followed by response. God wants to communicate with us; this is what we call revelation. God loves us, God always takes the first step towards us.

We are invited to respond, to cooperate with the love being offered. This cooperation, which requires trust, we call faith. As this faith grows it seeks understanding; this is what we call faith in the other sense of the teaching of the Church, the Catholic faith. The teaching and tradition of the Church offer us a rich menu to choose from to nourish us in the life of faith. This is the how of being a Catholic today, how to grow in holiness, to participate in the work of building up the kingdom of God in this world, the kingdom of love, justice and peace. Our faith needs to be known, celebrated, lived and translated into prayer. By partaking of the daily bread of sacred scripture, the liturgy (especially the Eucharist), prayer, and a life committed to virtue, we will grow as Christians, we will be true to our common priesthood bestowed at baptism.

This book is not intended as an academic survey of the basics of the Christian faith. I've tried to make it personal. I've used scripture a lot, which I think we should. Catholics are making up for lost time, having let the prayerful study of the Bible disappear from our practice, until the inspiration of Vatican II brought it back to our attention. The chapters are deliberately roomy, a bit untidy. The rooms are not swept and clean. I'm not sure that's a good thing anyway. Come and see. Come in and wander around. Take your time. Make your own notes. See where the gaps are, ask your own questions. Join the conversation.

I hope your encounter with this book helps in some way to deepen your faith, to re-energise your formation, perhaps set you off on new paths of practice. The one thing I've learned about the how in recent years is that you just need to show up. The life of virtue by definition is a life of habit. This bread needs to be consumed every day. Exactly what the meal looks like will vary from person to person to person, although there will be some staples such as scripture and the sacraments.

I've also learned not to get overly stressed about ideas of "progress" in the Christian life. Our society is obsessed with measuring performance. The Bible talks about bearing fruit and we will if we believe that this is God's work, not ours. This is an invitation to a new way of being human and belonging in this world. Jesus Christ, the eternal Word of God, became flesh so that we might have life, and have it abundantly (John 10:10).

PART I
WHY?

"Why did God make you?"

Penny Catechism

Chapter 1

"In the beginning..."

- God the loving creator

In exile you see things differently. When you're removed from familiar surroundings, including your sacred places, when your most cherished beliefs don't look as secure as they once did, then you look into things a bit more deeply. This was our experience during the Covid-19 pandemic. We were in a kind of internal exile, on the unwanted margins of our lifestyle, not allowed to visit our churches, not allowed to leave our homes (unless we were a key worker), to travel, to socialise, to celebrate our festivals, sacred or secular. We asked ourselves some fundamental questions about what we believed, how we behaved, what we took for granted. We listened to birdsong as if for the first time. We looked up to the empty skies. Nature breathed a sigh of relief, granted a Sabbath rest from our incessant activity and polluting. We lost loved ones before their time, came face to face with our own fragility.

Pope Francis says that to enter into a crisis is to be sifted, like wheat is shaken to separate the inedible chaff from the wheat: "Your categories and ways of thinking get shaken up; your priorities and lifestyles are challenged".[1] He goes on to say that the basic rule of a crisis is that you don't come out the same: better or worse, but not the same. To be tested is to grow, to grow is to make choices, and in those choices our hearts are revealed. The Pope urges us "to dream big, to rethink our priorities – what we value, what we want, what we seek".[2] We are invited to imagine "better ways of living together on this earth".[3] Ours is not the first era in human history to undergo a crisis, or exile, be that internal or external. The Jewish people were exiled from their land in the sixth century BC. Babylonia was the regional superpower and in 597 BC its armies, led by King Nebuchadnezzar, besieged and destroyed Jerusalem. Archaeological evidence suggests that the city within the walls was completely destroyed. The Temple, the most sacred site in Judaism, was left in ruins. They did not blame God for this. One of the remarkable features of the Hebrew scriptures, or Old Testament, is the searing honesty of the people who wrote about themselves. They did not produce propaganda, or self-serving hymns of achievement, but self-critical reflections on their relationship with God and each other.

The writer of the book of Chronicles sees the fall of Jerusalem as a punishment from God for their behaviour. Zedekiah, the young king of Judah, "hardened his heart against turning to the Lord" (2 Chronicles 36:13). The heart is an important organ in sacred scripture and central to the concerns of this book, so a brief note at this point might be helpful. In Jewish thought, the human being is conceived as a unity, an animated body. The Hebrew word "nefesh" meant "person" or "self" – a "living being" (Genesis 2:7). When "nefesh" was translated into Greek as *soul*, it was an idea which was foreign to the Old Testament. There was no body/spirit dualism in Old Testament thinking. There was a person, animated by God, and the emotional, intellectual and moral centre of that person was the "heart", a word which occurs over one thousand times in the Bible. The *Catechism* says that "the heart is the dwelling place where I am, where I live; according to the Semitic or biblical expression, the heart is the place 'to which I withdraw'".[4]

The heart thinks, as well as feels, as well as makes choices. The heart is our moral and spiritual core. This is where the Lord looks. As the prophet Samuel said, mortals look at outward appearances, but the Lord does not see as we see, "the Lord looks on the heart" (1 Samuel 16:7). When hearts are hardened then relations with God and neighbour are closed off. The law of Moses warned against this: "If there is among you anyone in need,... do not be hard-hearted" (Deuteronomy 15:7). The *Catechism* goes on to describe the heart as, "the place of decision... the place of truth, where we choose life or death. It is the place of encounter, because as image of God we live in relation; it is the place of covenant".(5) A key dimension of being human is that we are relational, we are called to live in communion with God, neighbour and the earth. Our hearts have a homing device, a longing for truth. As St Augustine said, addressing God: "You made us for yourself and our hearts find no peace until they rest in you".(6)

So when King Zedekiah "hardened his heart against turning to the Lord" (2 Chronicles 36:13), he was breaking covenant, breaking the life-giving bond between himself and God. His example spread to the whole kingdom. The leading priests and the people were unfaithful, "following all the abominations of the nations" (36:14). They forgot who they were, turned from the Lord and behaved as everyone around them did. The Lord got tired of sending them messengers whom they ignored or abused so his "wrath" rose up against them and Nebuchadnezzar was sent as the instrument of his vengeance. The Church today does not believe that Covid-19 was some kind of punishment on the world for its wrongdoing (some believe that, but it's not mainstream Catholic thinking). But in the Old Testament, that's how they interpreted disaster, and disaster often followed a turning away from the Lord, a hardening of heart.

Out of a total population in Judah at the time of around seventy-five thousand, it is estimated that as many as ten thousand were deported to Babylon. The ones who were exiled were the elite and those who supported them: the priests, scribes, aristocrats, civil servants, the ones who ran the country, the guardians of its self-understanding. These were the ones, in the books of Chronicles, who turned from the Lord. They were taken to Babylon, in chains, an 800-mile trek through desert and rough terrain. There are no records of how many survived the journey. We can only imagine the state of the exiles when they arrived "by the rivers of Babylon" (Psalm 137) and sat down and wept when they remembered Zion (Jerusalem). They had been defeated, displaced, and marginalised. They became "servants" (2 Chronicles 36:20) to the king and his sons. Their God, who had chosen them and led them out of slavery in Egypt, seemed to have abandoned them.

Let there be light

And yet scholars believe that it was theologians from this broken group of exiles who wrote the remarkable story of creation that we find in the first chapter of the book of Genesis. In Babylon, the exiles would have come across the creation myths of the region, including the *Enuma Elish*, the Babylonian creation myth. The first Genesis account of creation was not written in a vacuum. It can be seen as a response to the world view around them, a kind of pastoral statement to the exiles in the face of despair. At its heart is a remarkable claim that God watches over creation, it was an affirmation that this God can be trusted even when all the evidence suggests otherwise. The people in exile found a deeper level of faith in a faithful God. They were sifted and got rid of a lot of useless material. They came out of their crisis with a deeper faith. They found good news in their darkest moment.

The vision of God presented in Genesis is dramatically different from the Babylonian account. In that, the world was made out of the struggle between opposing powers and it took form when Marduk, the god of light, split in two the body of the primordial dragon. The heavens and the earth were produced from the sundered body of the dead dragon and, from its blood, Marduk fashioned human beings. Pope Benedict XVI said that, according to this account, "at the very origin of the world lurks something sinister, and in the deepest part of humankind there lies something rebellious, demonic, and evil".[7] Only the king of Babylon, a tyrant, the representative of Marduk, can repress the demonic and restore the world to order.

What a contrast when we turn to the book of Genesis. It is worth reminding ourselves how it begins, to take our time to read the passage, read it out loud, slowly, and appreciate its extraordinary depth and beauty. Listen to the soundscape. What do you hear? It is not the noise of cosmic carnage and the death throes of dragons.

> In the beginning when God created the heavens and the earth, the earth was a formless void and darkness covered the face of the deep, while a wind from God swept over the face of the waters. Then God said, "Let there be light"; and there was light. And God saw that the light was good; and God separated the light from the darkness. God called the light Day, and the darkness he called Night. And there was evening and there was morning, the first day.
>
> (Genesis 1:1-5)

Out of the silence of the void comes the wind of God (in Hebrew *ruah*) sweeping over the face of the waters. Chaos is not given a name, an identity. That would be to pay it far too much attention. Perhaps the "darkness" is an expression of what the authors of the text were experiencing in exile. They find hope, good news, in God's creative presence and purpose. Then we hear the first words of God in sacred scripture. Not the decree of a tyrant, not an order, or a reprimand, but the creation of something out of nothing, light out of darkness, the first moment of creation: "Let there be light" (1:3).

And there was light. God creates by speaking. God's word is generative. Creation is meant to listen and answer, although our track record on that front is not good. The Bible in many ways is a history of us not listening, of forgetting the promises of God. But there is always an invitation to come back. At the heart of the Jewish faith is an invitation to listen. The *Shema Israel*, the most important prayer in Jewish life, begins with the word for "listen, take heed, hear" from a passage in Deuteronomy: "Hear, O Israel: The Lord is our God, the Lord alone. You shall love the Lord your God with all your heart..." (Deuteronomy 6:4-5). God authors life, but there is no authoritarianism, no demeaning role for creatures, such as you find in the other creation myths of the time. Quite the opposite, there is an invitation to be in relationship with a caring and attentive Creator. As the *Catechism* says, "God has no other reason for creating than his love and goodness."[8] This is our *Why*, in a nutshell. We are invited to respond to that love, with all our heart.

What the Creator has made the Creator declares to be "good" (Genesis 1:4). This was not the point of view of the other creation myths available to the Jewish writers in exile. Those myths were all about the gods and their tyrannical proxies on earth. They were about the power of kingdoms, in the heavens and on earth. The writers of Genesis had a new insight, a counter assertion. For them, creation had value in itself. Creation is blessed. God's first blessing is on the creatures, even before men and women (Genesis 1:22). Creation is a treasure of God. Creation *is* a blessing. It is embraced and guaranteed, as we see in the covenant with Noah after the flood (Genesis 9:8-17). As we see when God takes flesh and dwells among us. In Matthew's Gospel, Jesus casts a loving eye over the lilies of the field and the birds of the air which his heavenly Father feeds (Matthew 6:26). There is no gulf between the goodness of God and the world. There have been moments in the Christian tradition when the depravity of nature and the purity and otherness of God have been emphasised, but that is not the insight that the writers of Genesis arrived at in the experience of exile.

Let us make humankind in our image

Then in Chapter 1, verse 26, those theologians in exile describe the creation of "humankind". In the creation myths of the society around them, as we have seen, humans were made from the blood of the slain dragon. It wasn't a very promising start. The purpose of humans, in the *Enuma Elish*, was to do the work done by the gods, "so that the gods will not be required to labour for evermore".[9] The deal was that the humans would be the slaves of the gods and the gods could put their feet up. Creation is a means to an end, humans serve the gods and the gods "lord it over them" (Matthew 20:25) in eternal indolence. What we read in Genesis is a revolution in thought, a completely new insight, better news than a vision of human beings as slaves and chattels of the gods and tyrants. Again, the emphasis is on the speech of God:

> Then God said, "Let us make humankind in our image, according to our likeness; and let them have dominion over the fish of the sea, and over the birds of the air, and over the cattle, and over all the wild animals of the earth, and over every creeping thing that creeps upon the earth."
>
> (Genesis 1:26)

And so it was, God created humankind. No mention in this account of Adam and Eve, that's the next chapter by a different group of writers, probably writing before the exile. This is about humankind, male and female. In another remarkable counter assertion from the view of reality around them, the writers of this creation account say that humankind was made "in the image" of God. In exile, Israel resisted the temptation to be like the Babylonian religion and its images of the divine. They may have succumbed to such temptations before exile, but not now. God was not imaged in any of the empires around them. But in a breakthrough of religious insight, the writers of Genesis proclaim that there is only one way that God is imaged in the world: *humanness*. God is not imaged in anything fixed, but in the freedom of the human person.

Walter Brueggemann, the renowned scripture scholar, believes there is a consensus that "the image of God reflected in human persons is after the manner of a king who establishes statues of himself to assert his sovereign rule where the king himself cannot be present".[10] The image of God in the human person, as Brueggemann describes it, is a mandate of power and responsibility. But here's the rub, it is power and responsibility as God exercises power. It is the power and responsibility of love. The Christian tradition, as it developed the Trinitarian understanding of God, would regard "image of God" as about being relational, made to be in communion, as God is a loving communion of Father, Son and Holy Spirit. We represent God best when we are in loving, right relation with creation and our neighbours.

Having "dominion" (Genesis 1:28) over creation sounds like the language of the tyrant, but this is our thinking, not God's. As Pope Francis says in his ground-breaking encyclical, *Laudato Si'*, "Although it is true that we Christians have at times incorrectly interpreted the scriptures, nowadays we must forcefully reject the notion that our being created in God's image and given dominion over the earth justifies absolute domination over other creatures."(11) We read the Bible *whole* and any expressions of God's power need to be understood in the light of the New Testament and the way of Jesus, who came "not to be served but to serve" (Mark 10:45), to show us how to live together in justice and peace.

The dominion which has been mandated, if we take our inspiration from the whole of sacred scripture, is more like that of a shepherd who cares for the animals. The task of "dominion" is not about tyrannical exploitation or abuse, but about securing the well-being of a blessed creation. The task of the shepherd is not to control or dominate but to lay down his or her life for the sheep (John 10:11). Humankind is blessed by God and given the freedom to "be fruitful and multiply, and fill the earth" (Genesis 1:28). This God governs by gracious giving and bestowal of freedom and responsibility. Men and women are not slaves of God, but images of God, agents of God if you like. We are collaborators in the majestic project of creation. That is the foundation for a key concept in Catholic Social Teaching: *the dignity of the person*. In *Laudato Si'*, Pope Francis expresses this beautifully, drawing on the words of his predecessor, Pope Benedict XVI:

> The Creator can say to each one of us: 'Before I formed you in the womb, I knew you' (Jer 1:5). We were conceived in the heart of God, and for this reason 'each of us is the result of a thought of God. Each of us is willed, each of us is loved, each of us is necessary'.(12)

In this initial survey of the first chapter of the first book of the Bible, we can hear many of the keynotes of any approach to formation or growth in the Christian life. There have been times in the history of the Church when the emphasis was on sin and guilt, but if we begin at the beginning, the message is clear: creation is good, it is blessed; it is abundant gift. We are good, we are blessed, we are meant to be. We have a purpose on this good earth, a responsibility, a mandate from God. But we are not God, we are not in charge. While we are good, as the next chapter of Genesis explains, we are also wilful and flawed, with a habit of turning away from God, forgetting our place in creation and turning inwards, living on our own terms. We mess up, we miss the mark, we harden our hearts. We see this in our relationship with creation. We have not always behaved as if we were the shepherds.

Sean McDonagh, a Columban priest and eco-theologian, offers an insight into why, in our European culture, we have not cherished creation as we ought. He cites Sister Elizabeth Johnson, who locates the root of the problem in the dualism we adopted in our encounter with the Hellenistic (Greek) world. This is where the notion of soul ("psyche") first appears, as we noted earlier. This way of thinking, especially in the Neoplatonists, sees the world as a polarity of spirit and matter, with spirit closer to the divine realm. In the late Middle Ages, the distinction between natural and supernatural, designed to protect the gratuity of grace, focused so much on the supernatural that "the world became no longer a gift but just a given, a background for the human drama".(13)

This pessimistic view of the world deepened further during and after the Europe-wide trauma of the Black Death (1346-1353), one of the most devastating pandemics in human history. It is estimated that something in the region of one hundred million, perhaps closer to two hundred million, people died, around fifty per cent of Europe's population. McDonagh points out that "sermons in the wake of the plague interpreted it as a punishment from God".(14) We may not see Covid-19 as a punishment from God, but our ancestors certainly saw a destructive pandemic in those terms. The way to respond, according to the fourteenth century Church, was to double down on a spirituality based on asceticism, mortification of the flesh and withdrawal from the world. Creation, as such, had no value. If anything, it was the source of corruption and death. McDonagh finds this negative attitude to creation present in some of the prayers of the Church, for example in the missal of Pope Pius VI, which was used right up to the Second Vatican Council. One post-Communion prayer read, "Lord, teach us to despise the things of earth, and to love the things of heaven."[15] We pray as we believe.

This spirituality was part of my formation. I remember as a child sitting through thunderous sermons delivered from a high marble pulpit. The world was full of sin and temptation, the body was weak and inclined to sin, only self-denial and God's grace could wipe our souls clean and give us any chance of getting to heaven. The alternative was an eternity of graphically described torture in hell. The focus was all on our relationship with God. Relationships with neighbour came second. Creation was merely a backdrop. As McDonagh points out, the majority of Christians never thought it was wrong that forests were devastated, or rivers and oceans polluted on an industrial scale as a side effect of powering economic growth. There were always witnesses in Christian tradition to the care of nature, such as St Francis of Assisi, or the Celtic saints. Many of the monastic communities of Europe were leading centres of innovative agricultural methods, but that was not the mainstream way of thinking and when the industrial revolution scaled up for its great pillage of the natural world, with the consequent degradation of human beings, the Church took some time to find its voice.

Our common home

Today, creation is on fire. The earth, our common home is being desecrated (literally, to treat a sacred thing with violent disrespect), and human beings live in societies of epic inequality. Millions live in poverty and oppression and are subject to degrading working conditions which very often benefit the insatiable appetite of richer consumers. The blessed creation is ransacked for profit and pleasure, the images of God in many places are defaced.

One papal document which reflects the urgency of what is happening to creation (understood as human beings *and* nature) is *Laudato Si'*, in which Pope Francis addresses not just Catholics, but every person on the planet about the condition of our common home. He states bluntly that "due to an ill-considered exploitation of nature, humanity runs the risk of destroying it and becoming in turn a victim of this degradation".(16) In language previously not associated with papal documents, the Pope says that because of the hundreds of millions of tons of waste, much of it non-biodegradable, "the earth our common home is beginning to look more and more like an immense pile of filth".(17) Unlike natural ecosystems, our industrial systems, at the end of the cycle of production and consumption, have not developed the capacity to safely absorb and re-use waste.

The Pope points to the compelling science linking global warming to the concentration of greenhouse gases in the atmosphere (carbon dioxide, methane, nitrogen oxide and others) as the result mostly of human activity. A key driver of this is a model of development based on the intensive use of fossil fuels. Throughout the document, the Pope is adamant that this is not just about saving the planet. It is a question of social justice, it is about promoting human flourishing, "the intimate relationship between the poor and the fragility of the planet, the conviction that everything in the world is connected".[18]

We are called to a change of lifestyle in order to reverse this damage, to restore the bond of right relations between God, nature and our neighbour. A point which has been rediscovered in Catholic thinking recently is that the lifestyles of those in the richer sections of any country are only possible because of the poverty endured by those who do not enjoy such material goods. In the present model of distribution, the Pope says, "a minority believes it has the right to consume in a way which can never be universalized, since the planet could not even contain the waste products of such consumption".[19] Being a Catholic today, a socially engaged and aware Christian, involves examining our lifestyle: what we consume, how much we consume, why we consume it, how it is produced, how it got to our home, and the human and environmental costs of the process. The change of lifestyle the Pope calls for begins in the heart, since that is the source of the problem: "The violence present in our hearts, wounded by sin, is also reflected in the symptoms of the sickness evident in the soil, in the water, in the air and in all forms of life".[20]

We are blessed, we are good, but we are flawed, "wounded by sin". This is an insight drawn from the second account of creation, the story of Adam and Eve, which was most likely written before the account in Genesis 1, somewhere around 900-750 BC, when the Jewish people were scraping an existence from the rocky soil of Judah and King Solomon was building a great Temple on the backs of forced labour. We will return to Adam and Eve in the next chapter, but for now the definition of sin in *Laudato Si'* is helpful for those brought up primarily with the view that sin was about breaking rules, often associated with the body. Pope Francis says that the creation accounts in the book of Genesis suggest that "human life is grounded in three fundamental and closely intertwined relationships: with God, with our neighbour and with the earth itself. According to the Bible, these three vital relationships have been broken, both outwardly and within us. This rupture is sin".[21] When our hearts are turned to the Lord, we will turn in compassion to our neighbour and to the earth our common home and live in ways which allow both to flourish.

This violence in our hearts has resulted in a distorted view of creation as a commodity to be exploited, to be bought and sold for our pleasure and entertainment, as well as for our survival. The exploitation is always of nature *and* humankind, since one requires the other. The papal encyclical which inaugurated the era of modern Catholic social teaching was *Rerum Novarum* ("New Things") by Pope Leo XIII in 1891. The chief concern in that document was the exploitation of workers in the rapidly expanding industrialised world. In the gender exclusive language of its time, Pope Leo XIII states, "Religion teaches the rich man and the employer that their work-people are not their slaves; that they must respect in every man his dignity as a man."[22] We hear in this the keynotes of the Genesis account of creation, the rejection of the *Enuma Elish* vision of humankind as slaves of the gods, the proclamation of the dignity of the human person as a "viceroy", if you like, of the king of heaven. Therefore, "it is shameful and inhuman to treat men like chattels to make money by".[23] A more recent publication from the charity Together for the Common Good, states that "no political or economic power formed nature or human existence. Creation is not a commodity but a sacred inheritance, and we have a high calling".[24]

Creation is a sacred inheritance, and one to be shared. When Pope Francis in *Laudato Si'* used the striking phrase, "The climate is a common good, belonging to and meant for all",[25] he was drawing on one of the first principles of the social teaching of the Church: *the universal destination of goods*. I have to confess that this principle has passed me by for most of my adult Catholic life. I don't recall ever hearing a sermon on this, or thinking it was anything that should impact on the way I lived my faith. No wonder it's sometimes referred to as the "best kept secret" in the Church. If something is a secret, it's usually not by accident, since the revelation would be embarrassing and uncomfortable. But it's there in Vatican II, in broad daylight: "God has destined the earth and all it contains for the use of everyone and of all peoples, so that the good things of creation should be available equally to all, with justice as guide and charity in attendance".[26]

Pope Francis, in his 2020 encyclical, *Fratelli Tutti*, brought our attention back to this key principle. He reminded us that this thinking goes back to the early centuries of Christianity. The key insight was that "if one person lacks what is necessary to live with dignity, it is because another person is detaining it".[27] He quotes St John Chrysostom who said that "'Not to share our wealth with the poor is to rob them and take away their livelihood. The riches we possess are not our own, but theirs as well'."[28] This is a profoundly counter-cultural insight. The market-driven society we have been formed in and live in does not take that view. What we own is ours and our increasing tendency is to build walls around it to protect it from harm. The Pope invokes another principle of the Church's teaching which in many ways is the acting out of the principle of the universal destination of goods, and that is *solidarity*. This is about believing that we are in community with each other, that we belong to the same human family and have access to the same abundance in creation. Solidarity finds concrete expression in service, and as the Pope says, "service in great part means 'caring for vulnerability'",[29] which in turn means getting close, looking into the faces of the vulnerable. Critically, it is more than just "sporadic acts of generosity".[30] It means that the lives of all are prior to the appropriation of goods by a few. It also means combatting the structural causes of poverty, inequality, the lack of work, land and housing, the denial of social and labour rights.[31]

This for me is a key passage. To make any sense of the universal destination of goods, we must begin by applying ourselves to an understanding of how poverty is contrived in our society, which includes my role in that. How could the goods of creation be shared more equitably in order to better promote the dignity of each person? How could the rights of workers be improved for the same end? In a gig economy are we aware of the working conditions of those who drive the vans to deliver the packet of pens or the book we ordered for next day delivery? As many have observed, the pandemic shone a light on inequality and gave us a new appreciation for the necessary work of those who keep our society running: who deliver and process and sell our food and household goods, who clean our office spaces and schools, who tend our sick, who teach our children, who keep our communities safe.

In the exile of lockdown, new insights opened up, or old insights re-emerged, about how interconnected we are, about how fragile and beautiful our world is, about how the goods of this world are drawn so disproportionately into the enclaves of a minority whose lifestyle can never be universalised. As those remarkable Jewish theologians wrote in exile, creation is blessed, creation is good and we have a role to play, a vocation if you like, to be the ambassadors for God on this planet, to promote justice and a fair distribution of goods, to look after the earth our common home, and each other. Creation is not a passive system for us to use as we see fit. It is an abundant, diverse and beautiful gift of the Creator, a reflection of his goodness, as St Thomas Aquinas said so memorably:

> God cannot express himself fully in any one creature: and so he has produced many and diverse life forms, so that what one lacks in its expression of divine goodness may be compensated for by others: for goodness, which in God is single and undifferentiated, in creatures is refracted into myriad hues of being.(32)

Sabbath rest

When the Lord finished his work of creation, he did what we wouldn't expect God to do, he rested. In some expressions in the tradition of Christianity, God is a remote and static being, perfect in heaven. In the Hebrew scripture, God invests his energy, imagination and authority in the loving act of creation and is tired by the effort. God's third and final blessing is on the seventh day, the sabbath day, the day of rest. This was not just a kind of divine bank holiday, a time to enjoy yourself. It was blessed and made holy. There is something much more important going on here. In the *Enuma Elish*, the creation account ends with the founding of the city of Babylon and the creation of the temple, the place where the gods might be worshipped. But for the exiles, with no land or temple, it was time which came first. Abraham Heschel puts it this way: "The meaning of the Sabbath is to celebrate time rather than space. Six days a week we live under the tyranny of things in space; on the Sabbath we try to become attuned to holiness in time".(33) For Heschel, a world without Sabbath would be a world that knew only itself, or a distorted image of God in the temples of the world.

The market economy we live in, and which lives in us, depends on the generation of needs and desires. These are needs and desires we did not even know we had until we saw them in another, in the advert, in the car driving past, in the neighbour's new extension. We desire according to the desire of the other, in the succinct insight of the French thinker René Girard. And this desire, of course, is without end, literally insatiable. In Heschel's memorable phrase, "things, when magnified, are forgeries of happiness".[(34)] The endlessly unfulfilled offer of desire leaves us rest-less and results in anxiety, which Jesus will address in his teachings, especially in Matthew's Gospel. For Brueggemann, Sabbath is a *resistance* to a consumer market which has now colonised every waking moment. The 24/7 culture means we can purchase and consume what we want when we want it, with one click, or with a drive to the 24-hour convenience store, operated by staff for whom the hours are far from convenient. Sabbath is an alternative, and "the alternative on offer is the awareness and practice of the claim that we are situated on the receiving end of the gift of God".[(35)] This awareness of gift is what lies at the heart of the Catholic Eucharist (thanksgiving) that we will come back to in Chapter 6.

The Book of Exodus provides an even more interesting description of God resting on the seventh day. The Lord is reminding Moses of the importance of the Sabbath, as "a sign between me and you throughout your generations" (Exodus 31:13). The text goes on to say that "in six days the Lord made heaven and earth, and on the seventh day he rested, and was refreshed" (31:17). The phrase "and was refreshed" is an addition to the Genesis text. The God of Israel is again seen to be depleted in some way by the labours of creation, needing to be "refreshed", literally to recover a full sense of "self". The root verb here again is "nephesh" – the "living being" God made in

Chapter 2 of Genesis. God rests to become a fully living being again, restored, breathing freely. The market economy, which is not regarded by Catholic social teaching as an intrinsic evil, nevertheless when unconstrained can produce *"depleted"* selves, reduced by anxiety and the endless frustration of never having enough, or being enough. The market depends to a large extent on depleted selves to operate, it feeds on the desire it creates. The unconstrained market also depletes those who work for it, demanding more hours, more efficiency, less favourable terms and conditions.

In contrast, Sabbath rest invites us to be "refreshed", to be "*gathered* selves", in the term used by Brueggemann.(36) The gathered self of Sabbath refuses the anxiety and hyper-stimulation of the market and its products. The gathered self draws on a different kind of energy, authority and courage, refusing activity for its own sake. The gathered self asks a different set of questions, such as: what did my creator intend me to be, how am I living with my neighbour, how can I be more generative and generous in my living, why am I looking for happiness in the wrong places? As it says in the prophet Isaiah's great vision of abundance, "Why do you... labour for that which does not satisfy?" (Isaiah 55:2).

Pope Francis is thinking along very similar lines in *Laudato Si'*. For him, Christian spirituality offers an alternative understanding of the quality of life, one free of "the obsession with consumption".(37) He advocates a return to simplicity, moderation, being happy with little, "avoiding the dynamic of dominion and the mere accumulation of pleasures".(38) He paints the portrait of a Christian as one who finds satisfaction in "fraternal encounters, in service, in developing their gifts, in music and art, in contact with nature, in prayer".(39) In a language similar to Brueggemann's notion of the "depleted self" he defines happiness as "knowing how to limit some needs which only diminish us, and being open to the many different possibilities which life can offer".[40] For him, this is an "attitude of the heart, one which approaches life with serene attentiveness, which is capable of being fully present to someone without thinking of what comes next, which accepts each moment as a gift from God".[41]

A note on our relations with our Jewish sisters and brothers

Christian Churches share a common guilt and responsibility for anti-Semitism over the centuries. It took a long time for this to be acknowledged, but a breakthrough came at the Second Vatican Council with the document, *Nostra Aetate* (Declaration on the Relationship of the Church to Non-Christian Religions), which was approved for publication on 28 October 1965. In the debates on the document, the role of the Catholic Church in promoting or supporting anti-Semitism was acknowledged with remarkable candour. Robert Graham SJ recalls that Cardinal Bea, an influential figure at the proceedings, "admitted in an address to the Council that anti-Jewish ideas in Christian history had helped Nazism".[42]

The document itself, although it stopped short of asking for the forgiveness which many at the time were looking for, is now seen as an important first step in repairing relations between the Catholic Church and the Jewish community. One of the historical accusations against Jewish people which fuelled so much persecution was that they were guilty of *deicide* (the killing of God), and as such were cursed by God. The document makes clear that "the Jews should not be presented as repudiated or cursed by God, as if such views followed from the holy Scriptures".[43] In stronger terms, the document goes on to say that the Church, "deplores the hatred, persecutions, and displays of anti-Semitism directed against the Jews at any time and from any source".[44] At a stroke, any Catholic sanction for anti-Semitism was removed.

Since the Council, subsequent proclamations and events have extended the statements of *Nostra Aetate*, perhaps most dramatically in the pontificate of St Pope John Paul II. He was the first Pope to visit the Nazi death camp at Auschwitz, the first Pope to attend a service in a synagogue and the first to ask for forgiveness for the suffering of the Jewish people caused by Christians. On a visit to Israel in 2000, by then struggling visibly with Parkinson's disease, he inserted a prayer into a gap in the Wailing Wall, a section of the Jewish Temple which was re-built by Herod in the first century AD. The prayer read:

God of our fathers,
you chose Abraham and his descendants
to bring your Name to the Nations:
we are deeply saddened by the behaviour of those
who in the course of history
have caused these children of yours to suffer,
and asking your forgiveness we wish to commit ourselves
to genuine brotherhood
with the people of the Covenant.[45]

"Judaism sees only one world, which is material and spiritual at the same time. The material world is always potentially spiritual. For Judaism, all things – including, and especially, such apparently non-spiritual and grossly material things as garbage, sweat, dirt and bushes – are not impediments to but dimensions of spirituality. To paraphrase the Psalmist, 'The whole world is full of God.' The business of religion is to keep that awesome truth ever before us."

Lawrence Kushner[46]

"In this vision he also showed a little thing, the size of a hazel-nut in the palm of my hand, and it was round as a ball. I looked at it with my mind's eye and thought, 'What can this be?' And the answer came to me, 'It is all that is made.' I wondered how it could last, for it was so small I thought it might have suddenly disappeared. And the answer in my mind was, 'It lasts and will last forever because God loves it; and everything exists in the same way by the love of God.' In this little thing I saw three properties: the first is that God made it, the second is that God loves it, the third is that God cares for it."

Julian of Norwich[47]

"We need economies that give to all access to the fruits of creation, to the basic needs of life: to land, lodging and labor. We need a politics that can integrate and dialogue with the poor, the excluded, and the vulnerable, that gives people a say in the decisions that impact their lives. We need to slow down, take stock, and design better ways of living together on this earth."

Pope Francis[48]

SEE

What do we see in creation – understood as human beings and the natural environment – and the way it is used? What gathering of information would help our seeing?

What do we see in the use of natural resources in our community, our household, our lifestyle – have we calculated our carbon footprint? See https://footprint.wwf.org.uk

Can we begin to see from the peripheries of our world, as Pope Francis invites us to do? What is the impact of wealthy nations on the rest of the world?

DISCERN

In what we see, what do we think is of God, and what is seeking to frustrate his will?

What options would we like to hold before the Lord?

With whom would dialogue help us to discern? Can we make more time for prayer?

Do we feel the "gentle pull of the Spirit" within us towards a course of action?

ACT

What course of action do we feel moved to embark upon? What impact will our actions have on those who are poor?

What strategy do we need in our course of action? Who do we need to work with, in what ways might we be an obstacle?

Are we open to the gentle, encouraging voice of God (as opposed to the strident, insistent voice of rigidity) prompting us to modify our course if needs be?

Will we make time to rest, to recover ourselves, to review our actions over time to discern if they were the right actions, with the best impact, or do we need further seeing and discerning?

Creator God,

thank you for the abundance,

diversity and beauty of creation,

given to us to reveal your love

and to invite us to become your images

on this earth, creatures who reflect

your care and compassion

for all created things.

Give us the wisdom

to understand that the goods

of the earth are to be shared by all.

Give us the courage to examine

our own lifestyle and habits,

to see that to have more than we need

is to deprive our sisters and brothers

of a dignified life.

Chapter ONE References

1. Pope Francis, *Let Us Dream: A path to a better future* (London: Simon and Schuster, 2020), 1
2. Pope Francis, *Let Us Dream*, 6
3. Pope Francis, *Let Us Dream*, 6
4. Catechism of the Catholic Church (CCC), 2563
5. CCC, 2563
6. St Augustine, *Confessions* (London: Penguin Books, 1961), 21
7. Benedict XVI, *"In the Beginning…"* (London: T&T Clark, 1995), 12
8. CCC, 293
9. Timothy J. Stephany, *Enuma Elish: the Babylonian Creation Epic,* (<www.timothyjstephany.com>, 2013), 38
10. Walter Brueggemann, *Genesis Interpretation: A Bible Commentary for teaching and preaching* (Louisville: Westminster John Knox Press, 2010), 38
11. Pope Francis, *Laudato Si'* (On Care for Our Common Home), 67
12. Pope Francis, *Laudato Si'*, 65
13. Sean McDonagh (ed.), *Laudato Si': An Irish response* (Dublin: Veritas, 2017), 130
14. Sean McDonagh, *Laudato Si': An Irish response*, 13
15. Sean McDonagh, *Laudato Si': An Irish response*, 14
16. Pope Francis, *Laudato Si'*, 4
17. Pope Francis, *Laudato Si'*, 21
18. Pope Francis, *Laudato Si'*, 16
19. Pope Francis, *Laudato Si'*, 50
20. Pope Francis, *Laudato Si'*, 2
21. Pope Francis, *Laudato Si'*, 66
22. Pope Leo XIII, *Rerum Novarum* (New Things), 16
23. Pope Leo XIII, *Rerum Novarum*, 16
24. Together for the Common Good, <https://togetherforthecommongood.co.uk/leading-thinkers/the-politics-of-grace-and-place>, accessed 29 March 2021
25. Pope Francis, *Laudato Si'*, 23

26. Second Vatican Council, *Gaudium et Spes* (Pastoral Constitution on the Church in the Modern World), 69
27. Pope Francis, *Fratelli Tutti* (On Fraternity and Social Friendship), 119
28. Pope Francis, *Fratelli Tutti,* 119
29. Pope Francis, *Fratelli Tutti,* 115
30. Pope Francis, *Fratelli Tutti,* 116
31. Pope Francis, *Fratelli Tutti,* 116
32. St Thomas Aquinas, *Summa Theologica* (New York: Benziger Bros., 1948), Ia q. 47, a. 1
33. Abraham Joshua Heschel, *The Sabbath* (New York: Farrar, Straus and Giroux, 2005), 10
34. Abraham Joshua Heschel, *The Sabbath*, 6
35. Walter Brueggemann, *Sabbath as Resistance* (Louisville: Westminster John Knox Press, 2014), xiv
36. Walter Brueggemann, <https://m.youtube.com/watch?v=7rtvjnmjMCc&t=34s>, accessed 29 March 2021
37. Pope Francis, *Laudato Si'*, 222
38. Pope Francis, *Laudato Si'*, 222
39. Pope Francis, *Laudato Si'*, 223
40. Pope Francis, *Laudato Si'*, 223
41. Pope Francis, *Laudato Si'*, 226
42. Walter M. Abbott SJ (ed.), *The Documents of Vatican II* (London: Geoffrey Chapman, 1965), 658
43. Second Vatican Council, *Nostra Aetate* (Declaration on the Relationship of the Church to Non-Christian Religions), 4
44. *Nostra Aetate*, 4
45. St Pope John Paul II, <http://www.vatican.va/content/john-paul-ii/en/travels/2000/documents/hf_jp-ii_spe_20000326_jerusalem-prayer.html>, accessed 29 March 2021
46. Lawrence Kushner, *God was in this place and I, I did not know* (Woodstock: Jewish Lights Publishing, 2016), 11
47. Julian of Norwich, *Revelations of Divine Love* (London: Penguin Books, 1998), 47
48. Pope Francis, *Let Us Dream*, 6

Chapter 2

"The Word was made flesh..."

God with us, God for us

We are not God. This may seem like a statement of the obvious, but I think it's at the heart of what we're considering when we look at creation. Walter Brueggemann talks about a grammar of creation as follows: *Creator creates creation*. We did not make ourselves; we are not the subject of the sentence. God, the Creator, is the subject, the protagonist. His activity is summed up in the transitive verb, *creates*. It is an ongoing process. What he creates is creation, of which we are a part. We are secondary, there is a reality prior to us, on which we depend. This is not bad news, this does not diminish us, but recognises our place in creation. We are creatures. I don't think the word has recovered from Mary Shelley's novel *Frankenstein*. The central character, Dr Frankenstein, calls what he made from body parts, a "creature", among other things. The creature itself, in a line of great pathos, says to Frankenstein, "I ought to be thy Adam; but I am rather the fallen angel, whom thou drivest from joy for no misdeed."(1) The creature is driven out into the darkness, rejected by his creator, in a version of the expulsion from the Garden of Eden which offers little prospect of redemption.

In the Christian tradition, we are creatures of a loving creator. Perhaps we don't see it that way because we breathe the air of the Enlightenment, of which *Frankenstein* is a product. The Enlightenment was a broad philosophical and social movement beginning in the seventeenth century which pushed back against what it saw as the repressive forces of religion and monarchical authority. Freedom would be found in the self-defining autonomous individual, released from the spiritual and social fetters of the Church. The French philosopher Descartes put the "I" at the centre, with his famous dictum, "Cogito ergo sum" (I think therefore I am). We find the same sentiment expressed in many ways since, including in the poem known to many a motivational speaker, "Invictus", by William Ernest Henley, which ends, "I am the master of my fate/I am the captain of my soul".[2] We are formed in a cultural environment which assumes that we are an "I" which can define itself, its beliefs, its destiny, even its gender. The title of the 1998 album by the Manic Street Preachers, *This Is My Truth Tell Me Yours*, sums up perfectly the culture of self-orientation. The autonomous self claims to be the "master" of its spiritual destiny.

To believe in God, on the other hand, is to believe that we are secondary, dependent, contingent. This requires a kind of psychological reversal. This is the heart of the Genesis vision of creation. Many scholars believe that the second account, in Genesis Chapter 2, was written first, at the time of King Solomon around 970-931 BC, perhaps as a critique of overreaching royal power. Brueggemann comments that the text could be seen as probing the question of whether there are modes of knowledge that come at too high a cost, or "the extent to which one may order one's life autonomously, without reference to any limit or prohibition".[3] Genesis 2 does not have the same magisterial account of creation, but moves quickly to the creation of man, which again is worth reading slowly:

> Then the Lord God formed man from the dust of the ground, and breathed into his nostrils the breath of life; and the man became a living being. And the Lord God

> planted a garden in Eden, in the east; and there he put the man whom he had formed.
>
> (Genesis 2:7-8)

Man is "formed" in this account (or "shaped" might be another translation) from the dust, the clay of earth. To use the word "formed" suggests the close creative attention of the Creator towards his creature (see also Isaiah 29:16; Jeremiah 18:1). This leads us to a fundamental truth that the human being is not just the result of chance, but we have our origin and vocation in the loving intention and design of God. Our closeness to the earth is emphasised by the Hebrew word play of *adam* (man) and *adama* (earth). Our life principle is God, who breathed into the nostrils of the man "and the man became a living being" (2:7). We are breathed into by God, we are alive with God's own life. This speaks powerfully and poetically of the intimacy between God and human beings at the heart of our reality. Dust is often associated in the Bible with the finite and death, but that does not render us insignificant. The shaping hands and breath of God give life and form to fragile humanity.

God puts man in the garden and, in a different expression of the human vocation from Chapter 1, he is charged to "till it and keep it" (2:15). This is an even more straightforward commission to look after the earth. Then follows the creation of woman as the "partner" (2:18) of man, made from his side. The man and the woman, who in Chapter 1 were given the commission to be "fruitful and multiply", are here seen as "one flesh". There is a covenant between the man and the woman, between human beings and God. Indeed, the relationship between the man and the woman is seen as an image of the relationship between God and his people (Hosea 1-3; Isaiah 54). From the beginning, human beings were made to be relational. We were also given limits. Creatures are limited, defined in relation to their Creator. We were given the freedom to eat of the fruits of the garden, but we were prohibited to eat of the "tree of the knowledge of good and evil" (2:17). The consequence of violating the prohibition was death. The *Catechism* describes the tree as a symbol which "evokes the insurmountable limits that man, being a creature, must freely recognise and respect with trust. Man is dependent on his Creator, and subject to the laws of creation...".[4]

The wisdom of the world

Enter the serpent. In the tradition, this has come to be seen as the devil, but the text doesn't say that. Pope Benedict XVI traces the figure of the serpent to Eastern fertility cults. These fertility religions were temptations for Israel for much of its history, tempting it to abandon the covenant. The message of these cults, through the serpent, is "Do not cling to this covenant, which is alien to you and which imposes so many restrictions on you."[5] The serpent is the first voice in the Bible to speak *about* God, rather than *to* God. It is in a sense the first abstraction about God, treating God as an object. The serpent does not deny the existence of God, but presents God as a paper tiger, an idle threat, a force which denies human freedom. When Eve looks at the prohibited tree through the eyes of the serpent, she sees that the "tree was to be desired to make one wise" (3:6). The serpent was a symbol of "that wisdom which rules the world".[6] This does not mean that God wished humankind to be ignorant or superstitious, but to be trusting, to be in right relationship with him.

Sin is a concept which the so-called "enlightened" mind would gladly consign to the dustbin of history, a blight on human freedom imposed by a controlling Church. But for the

Christian, sin is a mystery at the heart of the human condition. The creation accounts in Genesis do not refer to sin, but the tradition of the Church has studied these accounts to gain an understanding of what has come to be called sin, our sense of separation from God. From these accounts, key figures in the tradition, such as St Augustine, developed the doctrine of original sin which states that the human condition is fallen because of the sin of Adam and Eve. Only baptism can provide remission from this sin, although the human condition remains prone to sin, which is known as *concupiscence*. In *Fratelli Tutti*, Pope Francis defined concupiscence as "the human inclination to be concerned only with myself, my group, my own petty interests".[7] Sin is being turned inwards, *incurvatus in se*, in the famous Latin phrase. Concupiscence, the Pope reminds us, has been with us from the beginning of humanity but crucially, "can be overcome with the help of God".[8] Christianity is not fatalistic. We are not enslaved to our selfishness.

Sometimes the language of sin can seem overly abstract and technical. The Church is concerned that the faithful get to the heart of these concepts. The *Catechism* sees sin as being about our relationship with God and damage to that relationship. Sin is described as "humanity's rejection of God and opposition to him".[9] Sin is most fully revealed in its being forgiven. Once we're on the other side of it, then the backward glance confirms what we've been released from. The *Catechism* says as much when it states that the human story's ultimate meaning "is revealed only in the light of the death and Resurrection of Jesus Christ".[10] When we know Christ as the source of grace, then we know Adam as the source of sin.

Pope Benedict XVI says that "at the heart of sin lies human beings' denial of their creatureliness, inasmuch as they refuse to accept the standard and limitations that are implicit in it".[11]

He observes that for the ten occasions in Genesis 1 when we hear "God said...", there are ten commandments, so the commandments are as it were, "an echo of the creation".[12] They are not arbitrary barriers to human freedom, but signs pointing to the meaning and purpose of creation, part of God's design, a design which will be fully revealed in the new law of love embodied in Jesus. The ten commandments mostly deal with relationships, showing that our fulfilment as human beings is to be found in loving and just relations with God and our neighbours. To sin is to want to do our own thing, to grasp, to covet what is not ours, with no regard for the purpose of God for creation. That first sin in the garden of Eden is when we human beings, tempted by the wisdom of the world, let our trust in our Creator die. All subsequent sin is a "lack of trust in his goodness".[13]

The fallen Adam and Eve are a portrait of the human condition, with behaviour we recognise all too well. They are ashamed of what they've done and try to cover it up, literally, with fig leaves. But the good news is that God does not abandon them. In a moving scene, God comes looking for them in the garden. They are in a place of shame, on the margins of God's intention for them. God always comes to the place where people are ashamed. In a moment which the *Catechism* describes as the "*Protoevangelium* ('first Gospel')",[14] God calls to them, "Where are you?" (Genesis 3:9). There are some who consider the Bible to be the story of humanity's search for God, but I prefer the view that it is more about God's search for us and his endless attempts to manifest himself in human history. The expulsion from the garden sounds like a harsh punishment for the sin of eating from the wrong tree. In fact, God has altered the original prohibition, which was "you shall die" (2:17) if you eat the fruit, or perhaps the point is that you will die spiritually if you look for wisdom in the wrong place.

It is also worth noting that before they leave the garden we have the tender detail in the story that God made garments for Adam and Eve "and clothed them" (3:21). This is an act of care, of restoring dignity. When we read the narrative of the Bible whole, we can see this in combination with other similar acts, such as when the father greets the returned prodigal son in Luke's Gospel (15:22) by telling the servants to "bring out a robe – the best one – and put it on him". The son, who has wandered far from his father's house and ended up in the far reaches of alienation (feeding the pigs), is welcomed back with compassion. His dignity is restored, a place at the banquet is prepared for him. God's intention is not to leave any of his children in the places of shame as some kind of punishment. In the story of salvation, God comes looking for us. Jesus says in another part of Luke's Gospel that he came "to seek out and to save the lost" (19:10).

In Genesis 3:14-19, what we find is not so much the punishments of an angry God as a description of the human condition, with its inclination to follow its own desires, to miss the mark, to go astray. Reading the text horizontally – in other words from the point of view of the authors – the Pontifical Biblical Commission suggests that this account is composed "with the intention of interpreting historical events in which one can or one must recognise that the sterility of the land is a sign of a divine curse caused by sin".[15] In other words, as we saw in Chapter 1, what is written can be viewed as a theological response to what the authors see around them. They are living in an environment where they are scraping a living out of rocky soil, governed by a king with an obsession for wisdom. This is the result of sin, turning away from God. It's not a vision of humankind fallen into an evil state. The Church insists that humanity has not been totally corrupted, is still good, but "wounded" and inclined to selfishness.

This lack of trust in God's plan for humanity results in recriminations and distortions in the human community, oppressive social relationships. It's only now that the man "shall rule over" (3:16) the woman. This is not the case when life is in harmony with God's plan. There is a sense of anxiety and fruitless toil in the depiction of human life. Walter Brueggemann sees the passage as a theological critique of anxiety. The root cause of the turning away from God was an anxiety that there could be more to life than the vocation, permission and prohibition established by God. One of the reasons God offers for not permitting Adam back into the garden is that he might "reach out his hand and take" (3:22) from the tree of eternal life and overreach his status as creature. It is this grasping and taking that is at the heart of what we call sin, the mistaken assumption that there are no limits to what we can possess or control.

We pursue autonomous freedom, but as Brueggemann observes, "freedom which does not discern the boundaries of human life leaves us anxious".(16) He believes that the attempts to resolve anxiety in our culture – which are largely psychological, economic and cosmetic – are bound to fail because they do not address the causes. The allure of power over others, profit, greed, consumerism and the so-called wisdom of the acquisitive society, like the serpent, seduce us into believing that there is security apart from the reality of God, that our hearts might find rest in such things. Jesus addresses the anxiety of humanity, especially in Matthew's Gospel. Anxiety, in the teaching of Jesus, comes from doubting God's providence and seeking to secure our own well-being. Failure to trust God with our life is death. Brueggemann sums it up as follows: "To trust God with our lives is to turn from the autonomous 'I' to the covenanting 'Thou', from our invented well-being to God's overriding purposes and gifts".(17) We have not been left on our own to work our way out of the state of alienation from God. We are not trapped in endless cycles of anxiety. We have a path to redemption, already indicated in Genesis by the loving care of God. This path to redemption was manifest in an even more astonishing way when God's own Word became flesh and dwelt among us.

What are you looking for?

The beginning of John's Gospel is the Christian account of creation. The first phrase, "In the beginning..." (in Greek, *en arche*) is a reference to exactly the same phrase in Genesis 1:1. John's community would have read the Hebrew scripture in the Greek translation, known as the Septuagint. Scholars have noted that the first chapter of John's Gospel and the beginning of the second are structured after the account of creation in Genesis 1. After the famous prologue, the Gospel continues, "The next day..." (1:29), when John the Baptist testifies that Jesus is the lamb of God; then "The next day..." (1:35), when Andrew and an unnamed disciple (assumed to be the Beloved Disciple, the author or eye witness of the Gospel), meet Jesus; then "The next day..." (1:43) when Jesus meets Philip and Nathaniel; then "On the third day..." (2:1) we have the wedding at Cana. If the third day is counted beginning on the fourth day, as was the custom, then the wedding at Cana is the equivalent of the sixth and final day of creation. John is making the point that a new creation is coming in, an abundance of new wine. In a moment of poignant detail, it is Mary, the Mother of God, who points out the deficit in the human condition: "They have no wine" (John 2:3).

The prologue of St John's Gospel is an extraordinary text, much pondered over by many through the centuries. Again, it is worth our while taking our time over a key passage of scripture.

Perhaps read it over very slowly several times, or write it out by hand:

> In the beginning was the Word, and the Word was with God, and the Word was God. He was in the beginning with God. All things came into being through him, and without him not one thing came into being. What has come into being in him was life, and the life was the light of all people. The light shines in the darkness, and the darkness did not overcome it.
>
> (John 1:1-5)

In a sense, what we find here is already there in the Jewish scriptures. In the Wisdom of Solomon, we find the figure of wisdom who "was present when you made the world" (Wisdom of Solomon 9:9). Where the Christian account parts company with the Jewish tradition, is in the remarkable proclamation that "the Word became flesh and lived among us" (John 1:14). The Word, through whom all things were made, became one of us, became incarnate. Here is the heart of the Christian faith. The "glory" of God, which was "tabernacled" in the desert among the people of Israel, which was found in the holy of holies in the Temple, is now manifest in a human being that we could see, touch, listen to, follow.

In the Hebrew scriptures, Moses was given the law, which was a first step, a pointer of the revelation of God. In the book of Exodus, God reveals to Moses that he is, "A God merciful and gracious, slow to anger, and abounding in steadfast love and faithfulness" (Exodus 34:6). John applies to Jesus the same phrase that we find in Exodus, God's job description if you like, one who is "full of grace and truth" (1:14). The Hebrew words behind the Greek of John are "hesed" (steadfast love) and "emet" (truth that endures). This is what we will see embodied and acted out in the life of Jesus. At his trial, without any understanding of the irony of his statement, Pilate asks Jesus, "What is truth?" (John 18:38). In his classical mind, truth is a proposition to be proven by correspondence to facts. He is unaware that the mocked and broken man in front of him is Truth.

In the prologue, John the Baptist testifies to his followers that Jesus is "the Lamb of God who takes away the sin of the world" (1:29). Sin is singular here, not plural. The purpose of the incarnation of Jesus is redemptive. The sin we looked at earlier, that state of alienation from God's intention because of our overreaching pride, will be taken away by Jesus. This can at times sound remote from our experience, something transactional which takes place in a cosmic realm and somehow we are better because it happened, with no requirement on our part to do anything. But all of this theology, all of these signs in John's Gospel of the holy one, the Word of God coming into reality, are brought right down into scenes of remarkably intimate human encounter. Two of John the Baptist's followers begin to follow Jesus, literally. They walk behind him. In a vivid scene, Jesus turns round and speaks to them. These are the first words of the Word made flesh in John's Gospel, and what are they?

"What are you looking for?" (1:38).

Jesus looks straight into humankind's search for meaning east of Eden. When they ask him where he is staying, his reply is one for the ages, for every follower of Jesus, or seeker after the truth, "Come and see" (John 1:39). It is an invitation to encounter, to presence, to conversation, in ordinary time.

When Andrew and the Beloved Disciple come out of their long meeting with Jesus, which we might regard as a kind of induction into the new creation, the time is noted. The commentators I've read don't seem to find any symbolic significance in the fact that John notes "it was about four o'clock in the afternoon" (1:39). If it's not symbolic, as so much is in John, then it suggests that it's *just* a memory. They looked at the sun in the sky and remembered the time their lives began to be turned around. Then we see the dynamic of discipleship. Andrew goes to his brother, Simon Peter, and brings him to Jesus. Jesus "looked at him" (1:42) as in looked into him, knowingly, lovingly, and re-names him: *Cephas*, which means "rock" in Aramaic, translated into Greek as *Petros*, or Peter. In John's Gospel, we'll accompany Peter in his vocation and see how he matures in his discipleship through mistakes and denials, in which there is hope for us all.

The Word through whom all things were made is intimately present in John's Gospel, without cultic ritual, or thunder. The initial sequence suggesting the new creation ends "On the third day" (2:1) at the wedding at Cana. The third day evokes the encounter with the people of Israel and God at Mount Sinai. Moses is instructed to prepare the people with ritual washing and abstinence, "because on the third day the Lord will come down upon Mount Sinai in the sight of all the people" (Exodus 19:11). The Lord appears with thunder and lightning, the people tremble. There are different traditions in the Hebrew scriptures, different authors, different phases of understanding God. Despite the insight of Genesis 1 and 2 that God is an attentive and loving creator, there is a counter-pull, a continual tendency to view God as dangerously holy, to be kept at a distance. This could not be further from the intimate encounter in the Gospel of John's "third day" when Jesus goes to a wedding with his mother and provides the first sign of the new creation coming in, abundant wine for the banquet.

In the encounter between God and human beings in John's Gospel, it is all happening on our level. God has come down from the holy cloud to open up a new creation. What is more, we are invited to participate in this, to become insiders, "children of God" (1:12). What is happening is not a spectacle for us to admire, but a new way of being and belonging in which we can participate. Christianity is not primarily a set of complicated beliefs to be assented to or understood, it is not an ideology. In the words of Pope Benedict XVI, "Being Christian is not the result of an ethical choice or a lofty idea, but an encounter with an event, a person, which gives life a new horizon."(18) Later on in John's Gospel, the motivation on God's part for this encounter is made clear: "For God so loved the world that he gave his only Son, so that everyone who believes in him may not perish but may have eternal life" (John 3:16).

Has no one condemned you?

The Gospels are full of encounters between Jesus and people, very often people on the margins, or those cast out from the community. One such encounter has always stayed with me. The story of the woman caught in adultery. Scholars seem to be unanimous that it wasn't written by John. It is presented in most Gospel editions in square brackets, with advisory notes. There is a sense of alarm around this passage of scripture. It doesn't seem to appear in manuscripts of John's Gospel until about the third century, but it was clearly popular in the Christian community, passed on in the oral tradition, perhaps in some written fragments. I love the fact that the sheer pressure of affection from the Christian community helped it to find a home in canonical scripture. For the last seventeen hundred years it's been part of the Gospel and it's an extraordinary story of God's mercy which I'd like to stay with for a while. It might be helpful at this point if you read it through yourself, taking your time (John 8:1-11).

For my understanding of the passage, I'm leaning heavily on the American theologian and storyteller, John Shea, and the commentary in his book, *Gospel Light*. Shea's approach to scripture might be deemed spiritual-literary, a kind of reading which in some ways goes back to the creative engagement with scripture from the earliest centuries of Christianity. This doesn't mean you have free rein with interpretation. We have the guidance of the Church's tradition of centuries of reflection and authoritative teaching. If we ever stray out of the lane, the warning light will come on. This does give us some room for prayerful engagement, for reading scripture as it might apply to us, in our time. It requires close reading of the text, and connections between passages, all through the lens of tradition, which limits the chances of drifting into self-indulgence.

Shea begins with a reminder of the story in Ezekiel when the *shekinah*, the glory or presence of God, left the Temple because of the sins of the people. This if you remember was where we started. This was the time of King Zedekiah just before the siege and destruction of Jerusalem, which was blamed on the violent and sinful behaviour of the rulers and the people. The presence of God leaves Jerusalem in stages, as if reluctant to go. It goes from above the Temple "from the middle of the city, and stopped on the mountain east of the city" (Ezekiel 11:23). The mountain east of the city is the Mount of Olives. God's glory leaves, although the people are never abandoned. There will be a deeper understanding of the glory of God in exile, there will always be the offer of covenant. But the full manifestation of the glory of God will be seen in Jesus. At the beginning of our passage, Jesus comes down from the Mount of Olives to the Temple (John 8:1). The glory has returned. It is "early in the morning" (8:2), a new day. What will unfold is a new relationship between the divine glory and human sinfulness.

It says that "all the people" came to Jesus. The audience is universal. Jesus is seated, the position of a teacher. Before him is humanity, the human condition, more than a specific group in time and space. We don't hear what Jesus was teaching, because there is an interruption, as often happens in the Gospels.

> The scribes and the Pharisees brought a woman who had been caught in adultery; and making her stand before all of them, they said to him, "Teacher, this woman was caught in the very act of committing adultery. Now in the law Moses commanded us to stone such women. Now what do you say?"
>
> (John 8:3-5)

The woman is *caught-brought-made to stand there*. These are verbs of power, control, dominance. Shea points out that what the scribes and Pharisees are about is "finding people in their sin and holding them there".[19] Indeed, this is not just the special gift of the scribes and Pharisees. It is a mechanism of the human condition. In every age, the group strengthens its identity and sense of its goodness and rightness by singling out another group or individual – the "scapegoat" – to be sacrificed, shamed, cast out, so that the group can unite again around its common values. The woman in John's Gospel is a scapegoat. She is held in sin by the group, standing "before all of them" (8:3). She is surrounded, trapped by the righteous stare of the crowd, an object of their desire not to be in the same position. The man involved in the adultery, whom the law also condemned to stoning, was nowhere to be seen. So much of our communal life is characterised by this holding in sin, which is perhaps why the risen Jesus makes release from it a keynote of his instruction to the disciples.

The question put to Jesus is a trap. The accusers have no sin to use against Jesus to put him in the middle, so they try and contrive one. If he supports the stoning, he is in conflict with the Roman authorities, who have forbidden the Jewish authorities from applying the death penalty. If he does not support the stoning, he is against Moses and the foundations of Judaism. But Jesus is never thrown by a question, especially the ones that come from places of fear or aggression, like this one. He bent down and "wrote with his finger on the ground" (8:6) while the question hung over his head. Our fixation over the ages has been, what did he write? But Shea points out that what was important was that "he wrote with his finger, he wrote on the earth, and he wrote twice".[20]

In the book of Exodus, the ten commandments are written "with the finger of God" (Exodus 31:18). When Moses descends from the mountain, he hears the noise of revelry coming from the camp. The people have lost faith and turned to idolatry, the ecstasy of the golden calf. In the biblical tradition, the covenant between God and his people was often described in marital imagery. Idolatry, therefore, is adultery, and Moses has caught them in the act. Moses *stones* the people with the tablets of the law, breaking them. Those who were "adulterous", as it were, are put to the sword, about three thousand people are killed. But what the scribes and the Pharisees seem to forget is that the story does not end there. Moses goes back up the mountain, pleads for the people and finds favour in God's sight. Moses asks to see God's glory, which God agrees to, but with a strange condition: "While my glory passes by I will put you in a cleft of the rock, and I will cover you with my hand until I have passed by" (Exodus 33:22). In the Old Testament, God is only seen in passing – the glory of God is overwhelming.

God tells Moses to cut two more tablets. So God writes a second time. But between the first and the second, the glory of God passes by and reveals the divine essence, as John noted in his prologue:

> The Lord, the Lord,
> A God merciful and gracious,
> Slow to anger,
> And abounding in steadfast love and faithfulness,
> Keeping steadfast love for the thousandth generation.
>
> (Exodus 34:6-7)

This does not keep iniquity from being passed down the generations; this is what is called in the Christian understanding "original sin". The steadfast love of God does not mean that human beings are born differently. There is still the inclination to grasping and turning from God. There is still the group mechanism of naming and shaming, of holding people in the judgement of sin. Shea says, "the way of the earth is the forgiveness of God meeting the entrenched iniquity of the people, the releasing God pleading with the holding people".[21]

The true interpretation of the Mosaic law is that God always writes twice. Between the first and the second writing is the reason for writing twice. There are no sinless ones, all are dependent on the mercy of God. There is an alternative to the holding stare of the crowd. The human condition is not condemned to endlessly futile recriminations and hostility. After Jesus has been asked, "What do you say?" (8:5), he eventually straightens up from his writing and says, "Let anyone among you who is without sin be the first to throw a stone at her" (8:7). The divine glory has found another way to deal with the sinfulness of the earth. In the drama of a real situation, with a hush falling on a crowd, a shamed woman held in the righteous stare of many eyes (in the background the sound of sheep that will be slaughtered in the Temple, the looming presence of the Roman garrison), Jesus holds a mirror up to the scribes and Pharisees.

He does not stare. He shows them their hidden selves, the selves they want to protect at all costs by catching and shaming the sinful ones. He breaks the fake goodness of the group. He exposes the sinfulness at the heart of their violent desires. When the penny drops, beginning with the eldest, they go away, unwilling to stay and hear more about the new way of being human. Jesus bends down and writes on the ground again. "Jesus writes with his finger: the sign of God's authorship. He writes twice: the sign of God's forgiveness. He writes on the earth: the sign of a universal condition."(22) Jesus writes on the very clay that God formed human beings from. He inscribes in the human condition once and for all the law of love. He does not hold people in their sins.

Then there are just the two of them, Jesus and the woman. The staring crowd with its self-righteous, violent intent, has dispersed, undone by the mirror Jesus held up. The woman has been released from shame. Jesus straightens up again and says, "Woman, where are they? Has no one condemned you?" (8:10). Some translations have the woman say, "No one, sir" but the Greek word John uses here is "kyrie" which means Lord, the Greek version of the holy name from the Old Testament. This indicates that she is speaking to the divine source, the one who formed men and women from the earth they stand upon, the one who will soon reveal what being a human being is all about. And it is not condemning. The condemning crowds and its leaders have drifted away. Into the chastened silence,

God speaks: "Neither do I condemn you" (8:11). There is no condemnation in God. In the beautiful phrase of Pope Francis, Jesus has "anointed her with dignity".[23] Maybe this story was wedged in here because in the next passage, Jesus says, "You judge by human standards; I judge no one" (8:15). What we have seen in this story is a dramatic illustration of the staggering mercy of God.

What we are invited into is a world of conversion without condemnation. The woman is invited to change, to sin no more. We are invited to walk without sin, we are shown a way out of the enclaves of the human condition, which we thought was our entire world. Jesus shows us the way of salvation, or liberation. The divine glory has returned. It has written the *truth of twice* upon the earth and a new temple of forgiveness has been built in the precincts of the old. Before long, Jesus will occupy the very space the woman occupied, the space of the scapegoat, the shamed one. He will be subject to the same self-righteous violence, he will take on the sin of the world and, raised by the Father's love, breathe into us the peace of forgiveness.

The turning point of history

What does the phrase "the Lamb of God who takes away the sin of the world" mean? There are libraries of theology devoted to answering that question and through the centuries different ideas have come to the fore about sacrifice and atonement. This is a highly complex area, but what has helped me in recent years is to stay focused on the one word which I believe sums up Catholicism: *Love*. In *Fratelli Tutti*, Pope Francis refers us to St Thomas Aquinas who described love as a movement towards the other "made possible by God's grace".[24] Love is not a feeling, subject to our emotional ups and downs. Love – *agape* in the Greek, *caritas* in Latin – is a theological virtue, a disposition made possible by God's infusing grace, which as we practise it over time deepens in us. It is a desire to seek the good of the other, *including our enemies*, with no agenda, no ulterior motive of reward or feedback. "Our love for others, for who they are, moves us to seek the best for their lives."(25) The most memorable definition of love is in the first letter of St John, which cuts through all our floundering words: "God is love" (1 John 4:16).

When Jesus became human, he didn't come to tell us *about* love, he *was* love: embodied, moving among us, on the road, teaching, eating, sitting by a well asking for a drink. The Dominican Herbert McCabe sees this love in its fullest manifestation on the cross: "The turning point of human history, the moment when we realized what we were about, the moment when we saw that the meaning of being human was love, was the crucifixion of Jesus".(26) Jesus had to die, because he was human. But did he have to die *in that way*? Couldn't we have had all the benefits of salvation if Jesus had lived and taught and healed among us and then died a natural death, quietly, on the banks of Lake Galilee? Crucifixion was an ignominious death by torture which the Romans reserved for slaves and rebels. It was public degradation. A curse. The Gospels don't go into the details. They don't have to. Everybody in the Roman world knew about crucifixion and probably walked under its grotesque display at some point in their lives on the road into the city. The crucified Jesus was cast out, like the "scapegoat" in the ritual of Leviticus which bore the sins of the people into the wilderness.

St Paul says that God made Jesus to "be sin who knew no sin" (2 Corinthians 5:21) so that we might be put right with God.

Jesus knew the full depth of the human condition, absorbing its violence and alienation from God. McCabe makes a striking connection between the crucifixion and original sin, which he says is exposed most fully for what it is in the crucifixion. If original sin is the primordial maladjustment, then "in the crucifixion of Jesus it is finally manifested that the maladjustment of man amounts to a rejection of God's love".(27) The sin of the world shows itself for what it truly is at the crucifixion and simultaneously is conquered. This might have been what St Paul meant when he said that "our old self was crucified with him" (Romans 6:6). It is just as we see the fullness of our rejection of God that we see the forgiveness of God and the pouring out of the Holy Spirit. In John's account of the crucifixion, when the soldiers pierced his side, "at once blood and water came out" (John 19:34), which we take to be symbols of baptism and Eucharist, the gift of God's enduring presence.

In St John's Gospel, the opposite of love is fear. McCabe comments that "the first characteristic of people deprived of love is that they are afraid".(28) To speak of the sin of the world is to speak of its fear. This is a condition we are all familiar with. McCabe uses the example of a child who has been deprived of love. They are insecure, defensive, suspicious. They need to justify themselves all the time, they can't admit to being wrong. They need flattering images of themselves, they find belonging and security in any group that defines itself sharply over against a scapegoat. "Those who are deprived of love cannot face the truth about themselves," says McCabe. "They prefer, as John puts it, darkness to the light."(29)

After the death of Jesus, the disciples are in a state of fear, hiding in a locked room. They do not yet know the liberation that the crucifixion has brought them. The risen Jesus comes into their midst and says, "Peace be with you" (John 20:21). There is no vengeance in the risen Christ, no acrimony, no tit-for-tat. How could there be? That is the sin of the world. Then Jesus says that he is sending them out. Whatever is about to happen to them must be taken to the whole world. Then he breathes on them, or into them, and says, "Receive the Holy Spirit" (John 20:22). Just as the Spirit of God hovered over the waters at the creation, just as God beathed life into Adam, the old creation that got so much wrong, so God's Word made flesh now breathes the Spirit of the new creation into the disciples.

And the Spirit of the new creation is forgiveness, a liberation from the enslavement to the old way of being human, bound down by fear and the need to dominate and possess. We have a remarkable role to play in this new creation. In as much as we open it up, it is opened up; in as much as we close it down, it is closed down. We can hold people in their sins, or we can let them go. We can take part in the enslavement of others, or their liberation. As the Pontifical Biblical Commission puts it, "the salvation of God, that is his forgiveness, is not received by a person unless that person forgives the brothers and sisters (Matthew 6:14-15; 18:28-35; Luke 6:37). Forgiveness is received in forgiving".[30] This is the new commandment, to love as Jesus loved us, in self-giving to the end. That is not just love of friends. God's love is not partial. What has been revealed is an expanded vision of love, a universal love, including love of enemies, something never before proposed in human history. What seems impossible to human beings is made possible through the gift of grace, the Spirit of God poured into our hearts. This is how we will be images of God in the world. This remarkable project of God, the opening up of creation, this coming into being through forgiveness and reconciliation, is what has been entrusted to the Church.

"Our sin lies in failing to recognise value, in wanting to possess and exploit that which we do not value as gift. Sin always has this same root of possessiveness, of enrichment at the expense of other people and creation itself. It's the same sinful mindset we were just discussing in relation to abuse. The sin is in exploiting that which must not be exploited, in extracting wealth (power or satisfaction) from where it should not be taken. Sin is a rejection of the limits that love requires."

Pope Francis(31)

"Jesus, God the Son incarnate, lived out his life and death in obedience to the mission given him by his Father. He was sent to be among us, *to be human*... He was simply sent to be human amongst frightened humans, distorted and twisted by sin... In obedience to the Father he was the first really *human* being, the first to live wholly by love, which is what being human is about. And so, of course, he was too dangerous to us to let him live. We got rid of him lest we should have to be human too."

Herbert McCabe(32)

"What then is the meaning of this agape? The supreme passage for the interpretation of the meaning of agape is Matt 5:43-48. We are there bidden to love our enemies. Why? In order that we should be like God. And what is the typical action of God that is cited? God sends his rain on the just and the unjust and on the evil and the good. That is to say – no matter what a man is like, God seeks nothing but his highest good."

William Barclay(33)

Redeemer God,
Eternal Word through whom
the world was made, thank you
for becoming poor for us,
for walking with us, teaching us
the ways of God, healing us, restoring
the lost and the least to dignity,
showing us love.

Open our hearts
to the new life you offer us,
freed from the futile path
of rivalry, vanity and violence.
Give us the grace and courage
to offer ourselves up as you did,
in love, on the cross
of our salvation.

Chapter TWO References

1. Mary Shelley, *Frankenstein* (London: Penguin Classics, 1985), 103
2. William Ernest Henley, "Invictus" – <https://www.poetryfoundation.org/poems/51642/invictus>, accessed 16 August 2021
3. Walter Brueggemann, *Genesis Interpretation*, 51
4. CCC, 396
5. Benedict XVI, *"In the Beginning…"* (London: T&T Clark, 1995), 65
6. Benedict XVI, *"In the Beginning…"* 66
7. Pope Francis, *Fratelli Tutti*, 166
8. Pope Francis, *Fratelli Tutti*, 166
9. CCC, 386
10. CCC, 388
11. Benedict XVI, *"In the Beginning…"* 70
12. Benedict XVI, *"In the Beginning…"* 26
13. CCC, 397
14. CCC, 410
15. The Pontifical Biblical Commission, *What is Man? A Journey Through Biblical Anthropology* (London: Darton, Longman and Todd, 2021), 86
16. Brueggemann, *Genesis Interpretation*, 54
17. Brueggemann, *Genesis Interpretation*, 54
18. Benedict XVI, *Deus Caritas Est* (On Christian Love), 1
19. John Shea, *Gospel Light: Jesus Stories for Spiritual Consciousness* (New York: The Crossroad Publishing Company, 1998), 133
20. Shea, *Gospel Light*, 135
21. Shea, *Gospel Light*, 136
22. Shea, *Gospel Light*, 137
23. Pope Francis, *Let Us Dream*, 123
24. Pope Francis, *Fratelli Tutti*, 93
25. Pope Francis, *Fratelli Tutti*, 94
26. Herbert McCabe, OP, *God Still Matters* (London: Continuum, 2002), 5
27. McCabe, *God Still Matters*, 173
28. McCabe, *God Still Matters*, 173

29. McCabe, *God Still Matters*, 174
30. The Pontifical Biblical Commission, *What is Man*?, 354
31. Pope Francis, *Let Us Dream, 24*
32. McCabe, *God Still Matters*, 35
33. William Barclay, *New Testament Words* (Louisville: Westminster John Knox Press, 1974), 21

Chapter 3

"Let the oppressed go free"

God in the world, the mission of the Church

In the first sentence of *Lumen Gentium,* Vatican II's Dogmatic Constitution on the Church, the mission of the Church is described as "preaching the Gospel to every creature"[1] and later on in the document as building up the kingdom of God which Jesus inaugurated, to work together for its extension and growth. This is the "kingdom of 'truth and life, the kingdom of holiness and grace, the kingdom of justice, love and peace' in which creation itself will be set free from its bondage to decay".[2] For a summary of the Gospel – the good news – *Lumen Gentium* directs us to Luke's Gospel, with its emphasis on good news to the poor and a mission to the lost. Jesus carried out the work of redemption in his earthly life "in poverty and persecution".[3] The Church is called to follow along the same path when it communicates with humanity. It is not "to seek earthly glory, but to spread humility".[4] This has not always been the path chosen by the Church. At times over the centuries, the Church has been too close to worldly power, in fact has *been* the worldly power, too much concerned with wealth and prestige. There have always been prophets to bring the Church back to a Gospel path, like St Francis and St Clare of Assisi, like Pope Francis when he said, "I want a Church which is poor and for the poor."[5] In the words of *Lumen Gentium*:

> Christ was sent by the Father 'to preach good news to the poor... to restore the broken-hearted' (Luke 4:18), 'to seek and to save the lost' (Luke 19:10): in the same way the church surrounds with love all who are afflicted with

> human infirmity, indeed in the poor and the suffering it recognises the face of its poor and suffering founder, it endeavours to relieve their need and in them it strives to serve Christ.[(6)]

Guided by *Lumen Gentium*, let us take a closer look at the announcement of the kingdom in Luke's Gospel, the good news to the poor, and find there the inspiration we need for an understanding of mission. Kenneth E. Bailey, a scholar of middle eastern New Testament studies, has closely examined the text of Luke 4:16-30, the most detailed treatment of the inauguration of Jesus' ministry in the Gospels, sometimes known as the Nazareth Manifesto. Bailey suggests that growing up in the village of Nazareth – with a population perhaps of around five hundred people, a small number of extended families – Jesus would probably have joined in nightly discussion with the *haberim*, literally "the friends", a lay movement at the time devoted to studying the Torah. Bailey says that in the Gospels Jesus demonstrates skills in the rabbinic style of debate that would have been nurtured in these groups. This may have been the origin of Luke's story of Jesus being found in the Temple as a boy, impressing the teachers. This also may explain why he was invited to read in the synagogue. It was customary for the worship leaders to invite a worthy person to read from the scriptures and comment on them. Jesus was given the scroll of Isaiah, whether by prior arrangement is not clear. The reading is followed by an exchange with the congregation, during which Jesus invokes two figures from scripture as heroes of faith and the scene ends with the villagers trying to kill him. What happened in that synagogue to cause such outrage?

Before looking in detail at the passage, let's re-cap on the context. Jesus had a powerful religious experience when he was baptised. He understood that he was the "Beloved" (Luke 3:22) of God the Father. The Spirit descended on him. He knows *who he is*, now he has to work through his historical mission, or *what he does*. This starts when he is "led by the Spirit" (Luke 4:1) into the wilderness. Here he will discover what his mission is *not*. The devil puts before him a vision of his mission which meant, in the words of John Shea, being "physically full, socially powerful and religiously safe".(7) The Son of God as a status conferring personal privilege. Jesus refuses this self-centred understanding of his mission; his "No" to this allows the Spirit to fill him more completely. He has been purged of the distortions of identity and mission and so it is that, "filled with the power of the Spirit" (4:14), he returns to Galilee to begin his ministry.

In the synagogue at Nazareth, Jesus reads from Isaiah Chapter 61. But the text is carefully edited. One verse is cut in half and an entire phrase from Isaiah 58:6 has been brought in. What is going on here? And why did the mood darken so dramatically? The problem might have been that Jesus reads, "to proclaim the year of the Lord's favour" (4:19), but leaves out the second half of the verse, "and the day of vengeance of our God" (Isaiah 61:2). That in itself doesn't spark the riot, but when Jesus goes on to provide two examples of faith – a woman and a man – from among the Gentiles, there is uproar. The standard formula would be to refer to Abraham, Isaac and Jacob as fathers in faith. The synagogue speaker would have referred to esteemed rabbis, or Jewish teachers, in his *midrash* or commentary on the scripture. Jesus does none of this.

Some historical context might help us here. There is no mention of Nazareth in the Old Testament. The settlement of the village was known to have taken place in the second century BC, when the Maccabeans conquered Galilee and wanted to "Judaise" it. When the Temple was destroyed in AD 70 (this was the final destruction, it would never be rebuilt), there is evidence that one group of refugee priests settled in Nazareth. This would only have happened if Nazareth was known as a religiously conservative, all-Jewish town, a kind of settler town in the midst of "Galilee of the Gentiles" (Isaiah 9:1, Matthew 4:15). The first three stanzas of Isaiah 61 offer a vision of subjugated and defeated Gentiles who become servants. The Jewish community would become rich on Gentile labour and devote their time to holy leisure. This was part of the promise of the messiah, according to this community. This is supported by the Targum version of Isaiah 61:6-7, which reads, "You shall eat the possessions of the Gentiles... the Gentiles will be ashamed who were boasting in their lot."[8] The Targum was the Aramaic translation of the Hebrew scriptures from the first century, which added many words and phrases to the text and provided an insight into the thinking of the community.

So when Jesus started reading from Isaiah 61, his audience expected one of their favourite texts with its vision of the subjugation of the Gentiles. But Jesus stops short at the very point when the "vengeance" of the Lord was promised. More than that, Jesus imports a verse from Isaiah 58:6, "To let the oppressed go free". The edited text from Isaiah which Jesus read was as follows:

> The Spirit of the Lord is upon me,
> Because he has anointed me
> To bring good news to the poor.
> He has sent me to proclaim release to the captives,
> And recovery of sight to the blind,
> To let the oppressed go free,
> To proclaim the year of the Lord's favour.
>
> (Luke 4:18-19)

When Jesus finished reading he said that *he* was the anointed one – Messiah – promised in the text. But this was not the messiah they were expecting. In fact, this is "Joseph's son" (Luke 4:22), they know this young man. One of the things you don't do in a village community is break ranks with the village values. That tends to get you cast out. Where was the vengeance, the victory over the Gentiles? What was this "good news" Jesus was proclaiming to the poor? Did the words of Jesus refer to liberation of the poor from the social and economic conditions that kept them in bondage, or was it the forgiveness of their sins? The teaching of the Church is clear that it is both. The *Compendium* tells us that salvation is *universal and integral*: "It concerns the human person in all his dimensions: personal and social, spiritual and corporeal, historical and transcendent".(9)

Bailey argues that the message of Jesus in this passage focuses on three things: *proclamation, justice advocacy and compassion*. Liberation is not just freedom from sin with no concern for social circumstances. Liberation is from everything that oppresses human beings. This insight was part of the Jewish tradition. There was a desire to fix social relations which had fallen out of kilter with God's intentions. We see this in Luke's passage with the reference to the year of the Lord's favour. This can be read as a reference to the year of Jubilee (Leviticus 25:8-24), in which every fifty years slaves were released, debts cancelled and prisoners set free. Whether or not this ever happened is open to debate, but it was nevertheless a vision of a great periodic re-boot when the land and social relations were brought back into line with the will of God.

The use of part of Isaiah 58:6 makes an even clearer case for justice advocacy. The verse in its entirety reads:

> Is not this the fast that I choose:
> To loose the bonds of injustice,
> To undo the thongs of the yoke,
> *To let the oppressed go free,*
> And to break every yoke?
>
> (Isaiah 58:6)

For Bailey, the act of compassion (opening the eyes of the blind) is placed at the centre of the rhetorical pattern of Luke 4:18-19; in other words, the greatest of these is love. Jesus sees the world with the compassion of God and reaches out to those who are suffering, as he reached out to the two blind men by the side of the road: "Moved with compassion, Jesus touched their eyes" (Matthew 20:34). Jesus shows a visceral love for humanity, especially when it is at its most vulnerable. Compassion is part of the Old Testament vision of liberation, but it is not fully evolved. There is still a place for vengeance on enemies. Jesus expands this vison by fully revealing to us the inner nature of God. We'll look at this in even more detail in the Reflection following Chapter 8, when we consider the Good Samaritan. Without love, the work of justice advocacy and the work of proclamation are incomplete and can veer off course, drawn by worldly or personal concerns. Love completes justice and embodies proclamation. Whereas Isaiah 61 promised material benefits for the believing community, Jesus is saying, "this is what you're expected to give, not receive". Jesus expands the demand of the law, bringing the teaching of the law and the prophets to fulfilment. In Luke's Gospel, Jesus is on a mission of human liberation, beginning on the peripheries.

Building a better world

A key feature of the Bible is God's concern for the poor, beginning with a people on the underside of history enslaved in Egypt. Because of this experience in Egypt, the Lord insisted that the people of Israel show a particular care for the vulnerable. The Lord "executes justice for the orphan and the widow, and... loves the strangers, providing them with food and clothing. You shall also love the stranger, for you were strangers in the land of Egypt" (Deuteronomy 10:18-19). More recently the Church has called this a *preferential option for the poor*, for "those whose living conditions interfere with their proper growth".(10) The whole tradition of the Church bears witness to this.

For the Christian it is a social responsibility which the social teaching of the Church connects with the universal destination of goods. In other words, the goods of the earth are meant for all. If some are deprived of their share, then that is not the will of God, or natural, but a contrivance of human beings, an injustice. The *Catechism* states that "those who are oppressed by poverty are the object of the preferential love on the part of the Church which, since her origin and in spite of the failings of many of her members, has not ceased to work for their relief, defence and liberation, through numerous works of charity".(11) "Relief, defence and liberation" sounds very much like compassion, proclamation and justice advocacy. Let the oppressed go free.

Two thousand years after that scene in the little synagogue in Nazareth, what is the role of the follower of Jesus in this mission of liberation, especially the role of the laity? *Lumen Gentium* tells us that "it is the special vocation of the laity to seek the kingdom of God by engaging in temporal affairs and ordering these in accordance with the will of God".(12) In other words, the *world as it is* needs to be changed, made more just, more peaceful, more loving, so that it becomes the *world as it should be*, which is the kingdom of God, whose seed and beginning is in this life. The followers of Christ have a part to play in making that happen. How precisely we enact that role will depend on the gifts we bring to the body of Christ. The gifts we've been born with, or have developed through education, animated by the Spirit.

The mission of the laity in the Church is not just to "pray, pay and obey" as the old saying had it, but to take the initiative in the transformation of society. Pope Paul VI, in *Octogesima Adveniens*, published on the eightieth anniversary of *Rerum Novarum* in 1971, put this strongly when he said, "It belongs to the laity, without waiting passively for orders and directives, to take the initiative freely and to infuse a Christian spirit into the mentality, customs, laws and structures of the community in which they live."(13) This is striking. Here is a Pope saying to the laity, just get on with it. The work to be done is more than just the relief of suffering. It is to raise a prophetic voice with regard to the way a community operates and challenge that when it does not conform to social justice. It is to spread throughout the world a new set of values, *Gospel Values*. These are not the values of the world, but the values of God, revealed in their fullest in Jesus Christ, the values of humility, compassion, justice, forgiveness. In Chapter 8 we will consider the *virtues* of the Christian life. Values and virtues are often used interchangeably. It might help to think of values as "held" by the community or institution (although a person may be known for their values, as in what they stand for). Likewise, while virtues might also be "social", by their nature as stable dispositions learned over time, I think it helps to regard them as "held" by the person, even though they can be developed and exercised in a community. The main point here is that the Church is called upon to spread the counter-cultural values of the kingdom of God. This means challenging and seeking to change social relations where those values are absent and people are trapped in oppressive situations.

The oppression of poverty is the result of relationships based on domination and exploitation, not on love and compassion. This is a feature of original sin, simultaneously revealed and forgiven at the crucifixion. As it says in the *Compendium of the Social Doctrine of the Church,* "God, in Christ, redeems not only the individual person but also the social relations existing between men."(14) Jesus died not just to take away my sins but the "sin of the world" which is evident in distorted and unloving relationships between people. The driving force of the transformation of the world is love, which is the reality of God, the ultimate reality of the universe, which in its social manifestation, as St Paul so memorably said, is patient and kind, and rejoices in the truth (1 Corinthians 13:4-7). St Pope John Paul II, describing the mission of the Church, put it this way: "the kingdom aims at transforming human relationships; it grows gradually as people slowly learn to love, forgive and serve one another".(15)

The question of how relations need to be transformed to make the social order more just has been a central concern of Catholic Social Teaching from the outset. What needs to change in the structures of society and in the behaviour of those who run them? Pope Leo XIII began this engagement in the modern era with a focus on the question of labour and the relations between workers and employers. While ahead of his time in many ways, he was also a man of his times. While he was concerned for the conditions of the working classes, he was not advocating radical change. He called for a just wage, dignity at work, the extension of private property, reasonable hours and decent working conditions. It was bold, certainly, and drew the wrath of many so-called Christian capitalists, but fundamentally he was on the side of order and authority. There was a critique of both liberal capitalism and socialism, but the thrust of his vision for a "just ordering" was for a more restrained, or humanised, capitalism.

The approach of Leo XIII was that of the concerned patrician who was mindful of the spiritual and corporeal needs of ordinary people, a sense of knowing what was best for them. Part of the responsibility of employers was to make sure their workers were not exposed to "corrupting influences".[(16)] This approach evolved in the teaching of subsequent popes. Paul VI, in his 1967 social encyclical, *Populorum Progressio*, calls for a solidarity with the poor which "would allow all peoples to become the artisans of their destiny".[(17)] This is a key shift. No longer is the approach that "we", who are discerning and knowledgeable, tell "them" (the poor) what they need in order to live a better life, or worse still provide immediate relief from misery but do little to change the conditions that put them in poverty in the first place. We are called to empower and facilitate, to contribute to situations where those who are oppressed by poverty have a voice and are at the heart of any solutions which are proposed.

If justice describes the circumstances in which each person receives what is his or her due, then what is "due" to each person, what does human flourishing look like, and what kind of structures in society can bring that about? *Gaudium et Spes* (The Pastoral Constitution on the Church in the Modern World) takes as a starting point the "exceptional dignity which belongs to the human person",[(18)] which we traced back to the book of Genesis and the creation of human beings in the image of God. Because of this dignity, "the rights and duties" of the human person "are universal and inviolable".[(19)] In the immediate post-

War period, Catholic thinkers were central to the drawing up of the UN Declaration of Human Rights.

In the subsequent decades the Church emphasised that the integral development of the human person was very much its concern: the development of the whole person and every person. This is Christian humanism. As the *Compendium* defines it, "the liberation from everything that oppresses man".[20] *Gaudium et Spes* stipulates that a "truly human life" consists of

> food, clothing, shelter, the rights of free choice of one's state of life and to found a family, to education, to work, to one's good name, to respect, to appropriate information, to act in accordance with the right norm of conscience, to the protection of one's private life and to a just freedom, including religious freedom.[21]

This is the Church fully engaged in the question of what human flourishing looks like in this life. There are those in the Church today who would argue that the Church's priority is the "care of souls" and the "salvation" of each person, which means dying in a state of grace sufficient to get to heaven. The social teaching of the Church in recent years does not deny any of this, but what this teaching makes clear is that salvation is universal and integral. It concerns the human person in all their dimensions, social as well as personal, corporeal as well as spiritual.

Catholics are encouraged, indeed expected, to show a compassionate interest in the social order and its progress. The Church no longer sees itself as "an island of grace in a world of sin",[22] as Robert Calderisi characterises the stance before Vatican II, but as a promoter of the progress and development of humanity. The social order, states *Gaudium et Spes*, should "favour the good of people".[23] The social order needs to continually evolve to ensure that violations of human dignity are challenged and removed and the circumstances for a truly human life are increasingly in place. This is a social order "founded on truth, built in justice and animated by love".[24] It is not a given that history will tend in this direction. The Church's vision of this life is not utopian. Its teaching on original sin provides a healthy realism that wherever society seems to be advancing, the inclination to greed and exploitation is always present. To achieve the just society envisaged in the document requires "renewal of minds and major changes in society".[25]

This line of thought develops through the teaching of the popes, with the significant introduction by St John Paul II of the concept of "structures of sin" in *Sollicitudo Rei Socialis* ("On Social Concern"). This is the insight that the economic and social system itself and the relationships it allows, can be a source of sin and should be a matter for reform. Structural sin is not a vague sense that the system is to blame and no one person is at fault. It is rooted in personal sin, since the characteristics of structural sin – "desire for profit" and "the thirst for power"[26] – come from the human heart. This *libido dominandi* or desire to dominate others, St Augustine traces back to one of the consequences of original sin. The structures in society which arise from this desire are presented by those who run them as normative and resistant to radical challenge. Exposing the structures of sin – revealing what is hidden in plain sight – is part of this mission.

The response to structures of sin proposed by St Pope John Paul II is the "virtue" of solidarity. He stresses that this is "not a feeling of vague compassion" but is "a firm and persevering determination to commit oneself to the common good",[27] which is to say the good of all, especially those who are poor. What hinders human flourishing is the thirst for power, the desire to impose our will on others, to exploit and dominate. The opposing attitude, found in the Gospel, is to "lose oneself" for the sake of our neighbour, "to serve him instead of oppressing him for one's own advantage".[28] The Church's vision is for *structures of solidarity*, not structures of sin. The teaching of social doctrine (Catholic social teaching) is part of the Church's evangelising mission and since it is aimed at guiding behaviour it gives rise to a "commitment to justice" according to each individual's "role, vocation and circumstances".[29] The motivation for this "social evangelisation" is concern for the poor which "must be translated at all levels into concrete actions, until it decisively attains a series of necessary reforms".[30]

As St Paul said to the community in Corinth, "there are varieties of gift, but the same Spirit" (1 Corinthians 12:4). There is a variety of activities, "but it is the same God who activates all of them in everyone" (1 Corinthians 12:6). We're each given a "manifestation of the Spirit for the common good" (1 Corinthians 12:7). For some it will be the kindness and people skills involved in visiting an elderly and isolated person at home; for others it will be using teaching skills as a catechist; for others using social and organisational skills to run a parish lunch; for others it might be the planning and teamwork required to offer a refugee family settled status; for others still it might be advocating at regional or even national level with detailed, compelling arguments for changing some aspect of legislation to make the law more humane. As it suggests in the Parable of the Talents (Matthew 25:14-30), we do what we can with the gifts we have.

The *Compendium* describes the social doctrine of the Church as a "work site", a work in progress, "where perennial truth penetrates and permeates new circumstances".[31] In a remarkable way, beginning with Pope Leo XIII, the teaching of the Church entered into the "sphere of practice", the realm of social realities, which are ever changing and never exhausted by analysis. The social teaching of the Church since Leo XIII has had a firm focus on relations in society which are unjust, which reduce some people to a less than truly human life. What has come more and more into sharp focus is the response required of those in the Church. Pope Francis, in his encyclical *Evangelii Gaudium*, says that "Each individual Christian and every community is called to be an instrument of God for the liberation and promotion of the poor, and for enabling them to be fully a part of society."[32] This work, which is born of the liberating action of grace within each of us, means "working to eliminate the structural causes of poverty" as well as "small daily acts of solidarity in meeting the needs which we encounter".[33]

The good news is that we are loved by God, our creator; we are not slaves, we are friends. This does not change our status as creatures but it bestows on creatures a remarkable dignity. We are loved and we have been invited to receive God's love and love him in return. Jesus, by his teaching, death and resurrection, has shown us a way out of the bondage of original sin and its personal and social consequences. We can be liberated from this condition, which while it is not evil, often results in consequences of misery for ourselves and others. Being a Christian is not a private matter. When we respond to the forgiveness of God, and the invitation to life in the new creation, it "brings forth in our lives and actions a primary and fundamental response: to desire, seek and protect the good of others".[34] The kerygma, says Pope Francis, has a clear social content: "at the very heart of the Gospel is life in community and engagement with others".[35] He sums it up as follows: "It is no longer possible to claim that religion should be restricted to the private sphere and that it exists only to prepare souls for heaven".[36] God wants his children to be happy in this world. One of the injunctions of the Lord's Prayer, after all, is for the Father's will to be done *"on earth* as it is in heaven" (Matthew 6:10).

Building on the teaching of his predecessors, Pope Francis calls us to be "with" those who are poor, accompanying them in their struggle for liberation, helping to amplify their voice, their story, their account of their circumstances and what needs to be learned so that it is not forever repeated. He calls for a Church of encounter and service; a Church of reality, not ideas; of nouns, not adjectives; of time, not place. A Church of compassion and justice advocacy, which proclaims the good news of God, a Church "that goes forth from its sacristies, in order to accompany life, to sustain hope, to be the sign of unity... to build bridges, to break down walls, to sow seeds of reconciliation".[37]

Love in action

There is of course "bad news" in the Church as well, and in recent years we have heard a great deal of it, especially relating to child sex abuse scandals and the institutional inertia in responding effectively. This should never be passed over, or denied, or played down. Anyone connected to the Church must commit to an exemplary standard of safeguarding. This is another dimension of social justice and the promotion of right relations. On the other hand, we should not allow the "bad news" to overwhelm the generations of "good news" in the Church. There are many millions of ordinary Catholics who perform unseen acts of kindness and charity every day, standing up for the oppressed and walking with them towards a better life.

On a global scale, the Caritas Internationalis network of the Catholic Church is one of the largest humanitarian organisations in the world. According to Robert Calderisi, "the Catholic humanitarian and development network Caritas spends about $3 billion a year and is the largest private charity in the world after the International Red Cross".[38] Caritas Internationalis is a confederation of over 160 member organisations – including, in Britain and Ireland, Catholic Aid For Overseas Development (CAFOD), Caritas Social Action Network (CSAN), Scottish Catholic International Aid Fund (SCIAF) and Trocaire – who work at the grassroots in almost every country of the world. When a crisis hits, Caritas is there on the ground, the Church showing the face of Christ to the most stricken. Inspired by the Catholic faith, Caritas is the helping hand of the Church, reaching out to the poor, vulnerable and excluded, regardless of race or religion, to build a world based on justice and fraternal love.

Caritas is not the full extent of the Church's service to the world. According to Calderisi,

> Those services are provided in 140,000 schools, 5,500 hospitals and 18,000 clinics around the world, not to mention 16,000 homes for the elderly and handicapped, 10,000 orphanages, 12,000 nurseries, and 37,000 centers of informal education. Some 65 percent of Catholic hospitals are located in developing countries.[39]

If we zoom in on one region, in Kerala, India, the Trivandrum Social Service Society (the local Caritas), "trains leaders of 1,200 self-help groups, supports fifty women's forums in combating alcoholism and domestic violence, lends money to 4,000 women fish vendors, helps set up unions, and offers scholarships to Dalit (Untouchables)".[40]

Closer to home, in my role with Caritas Social Action Network, I work with over fifty charities in England and Wales, with thousands of paid staff and many more volunteers, who every day are engaged on the front line of poverty and disadvantage, advocating for a more just and humane society. In the pandemic, that need was more acute and the response of the charities more urgent, more creative, more invested in advocating for structural change. To name just a few: the Jesuit Refugee Service which accompanies and advocates on behalf of refugees seeking sanctuary in Britain faced with a hostile system; the women@thewell charity in London which offers shelter, support and a way out for women and girls trapped in prostitution and sex trafficking; the Prison Advice and Care Trust (PACT) which provides support for prisoners and their families and advocates for a humane criminal justice system; or the St Vincent de Paul Society (SVP), with around ten thousand volunteers, a cohort of compassion, befriending isolated and excluded people.

I have been fortunate to work with and visit some inspirational examples of caritas in action. Fatima House in Birmingham is a former presbytery from the days when parishes had six or seven priests serving a large Catholic population. The one priest left in the large parish house, inspired by Pope Francis, transformed the place into a refuge for destitute female asylum seekers. These are women who have often been abused, exploited and trafficked. Many do not speak English and often they are separated from their children. They are destitute because they have been refused asylum in a system which is deliberately hostile to refugees. When their case has been refused they have no access to public funds. They are on the very margins of viable life.

Fatima House is run by two lay Columban missionaries, Mauricio and Nathalie. When a group of us visited, we prayed with them and shared a simple meal and talked about the project. We didn't meet any of the women the house serves.

Their privacy is paramount. Most of the women are Muslim so out of respect to them, the only room with any Catholic imagery was the small sitting room where we met. This was just one example among thousands of a key feature of the Church's outreach to the vulnerable: *gratuity*. What is given is given in love, freely. As Benedict XVI said in *Deus Caritas Est*, charity is not a means of engaging in proselytism, or trying to convert people to Christianity in exchange for services: "Love is free; it is not practised as a way of achieving other ends".(41) Mauricio and Nathalie were the face of Christ to those vulnerable and rejected women and at the same time, although they only said this to us, not them, in the women they served they encountered Christ, as truly as they encountered him in the Eucharist or the word of God.(42)

What has been created in places like Fatima House is community, an intentional community which resembles the kingdom of God. It is a community of welcome, generosity and compassion. It is being together the way Jesus taught his disciples to be together, not in rivalry, not wasting time about arguing who is the greatest, not lording it over each other, not obsessing about prestige and possessions. This, for Pope Francis, is what the kerygma, the essence of Christianity, is about. "At the very heart of the Gospel is life in community and engagement with others. The content of the first proclamation has an immediate moral implication centred on charity."(43) Places like Fatima House show what this looks like in practice. To be there is to be moved, to feel the Spirit of God at work in the world. This is the kind of structure of solidarity by which the Church responds to the structures of sin.

Another example, which had a profound impact on me, was a visit to the Philippines with a group of headteachers a few years ago. We visited one of the largest cemeteries in Manila, an old-style Spanish colonial cemetery, with wall niches for graves and large family canopies and tombstones, all in old marble or more recent whitewashed concrete. We were told that the poorest of the poor lived there, entire families, a community of people on the very edge of life. We walked around, like self-conscious tourists. In the tomb-canopies, families had made homes: washing hung out to dry, meals were being prepared on portable stoves, there were plastic chairs, mats to sleep on, toddlers running around. I passed a group of men sitting on a large tombstone, drinking pink liquid from a plastic bottle. One of them caught my eye and said, "sorry about this", his hand indicating the bottle, the drinking. I was lost for words and think I managed to say, "there's no need to apologise to me". If I'd thought about it deeply enough, it should have been me offering them an apology.

Then we heard the children from a distance, singing, chanting, laughing. When we got close, we found them inside one of the big concrete open-sided canopies. Two women were with them, from the local parish. They came and offered the children rudimentary classes. They had no resources, no books, or computers, or whiteboards, but education has been going on much longer than these devices have been around. They were telling them stories, teaching them songs about basic hygiene, safety on the streets, the danger of inhaling solvents. These children were literally living among the dead, but had been found and were being offered a helping hand, as were their parents in other ways. A chance to be liberated from dehumanising conditions. I was distressed by what I saw in that cemetery but also inspired that I found the Church there, where it needed to be, accompanying and serving, encountering her Lord in society's discarded ones. In these examples of love in action – in Kerala, in Fatima House, in a cemetery in Manila – dignity was being restored to the oppressed, hope was blooming in the darkest of places. This was the mission of the Church, on the margins, bringing good news to the poor.

In the upper room in Jerusalem, the risen Jesus breathed the Spirit of the new creation, the Spirit of forgiveness and liberation, into frightened disciples who were "locked" in the old creation of Adam. This is the good news of our salvation, an invitation to become fully human which passes through forgiveness, the first effect of the gift of love. Not through any merit on our part; this is all gift. We are receivers, through faith, we are invited to be co-creators, through grace.

In Luke's account, the Holy Spirit was sent on the day of Pentecost, when the Church was openly seen by the crowds and the spread of the Gospel among all the nations of the earth began. The Holy Spirit "builds, animates and sanctifies the Church"[(44)] for its mission of proclaiming and establishing the kingdom of God. In this mission the Church should be characterised by the "charity, humility and self-denial"[(45)] of its founder Jesus Christ. Its members will bear fruit by the power of the Holy Spirit, each according to their ability. "Each Christian and every community must discern the path that the Lord points out, but all of us are asked to obey his call to go forth from our own comfort zone in order to reach all the 'peripheries' in need of the light of the Gospel."[(46)]

Jesus was not Spartacus

I'm not suggesting that the mission of the Church is purely social, as if we were some global INGO (International Non-Governmental Organisation) committed to human liberation. There are many organisations committed to justice which have no foundation in the Gospel, whose members also act with compassion and are motivated by justice. The difference lies in the source of this compassion. Benedict XVI said that those who work for the Church's charitable organisations (and I would say this applies to all Christians) need "a formation of the heart: they need to be led to that encounter with Christ which awakens their love and opens their spirit to others".[47]

The Christian, in other words, is powered by grace, the life of the Spirit of God in them, not by their own desire to make the world a better place. The Christian completes justice with love, seeing in the vulnerable one the face of Christ, seeing in the vulnerable one's circumstances an affront to justice which needs to be challenged and changed, seeing the vulnerable as agents of their own betterment, as people who have a voice in what is good for them and not just objects of charity.

Pope Benedict XVI said that the Church's deepest nature is expressed in a three-fold ministry: "proclaiming the word of God (*kerygma-martyria*), celebrating the sacraments (*leitourgia*), and exercising the ministry of charity (*diakonia*). These duties presuppose each other and are inseparable". He does go on to say, however, that "For the Church, charity is not a kind of welfare activity which could equally well be left to others, but is a part of her nature, an indispensable expression of her very being."[48] The more closely we look at the three-fold ministry outlined by Benedict, the more clearly we see that there is a social dimension at the heart of each of them: the proclamation of good news to the poor, the ministry of charity and, as we'll explore in Chapter 6 on the Eucharist, the broken body of the Lord identified with the last and the least.

In the next chapter we will begin to explore in more detail what the Gospel's call to personal "metanoia" or change might look like and in subsequent chapters how this new life might be nourished and sustained. Our motivation for changing the world is not an act of will, like going on a diet, or training for a marathon. What drives us is grace, the love of God poured into our hearts by the Holy Spirit (Romans 5:5), accessed through prayer, scripture and liturgy, primarily the Eucharist. God loves the world and wants us to be the ambassadors for that love, the means by which he hears the voice of the poor and works for their liberation.

We are not seeking to overthrow the state and replace it with the Church. As Pope Benedict said, "Jesus was not Spartacus",(49) he did not come to lead a violent revolution against injustice. There was no violence in him, only love. He came to bring us closer to God, to give us hope, to show us a more loving way of being together. Christians are committed to the transformation of the world, but peacefully, persuasively, by example, mostly at a local level by what Francis calls "people building", being catalysts for the transformation of social relationships, advocating more just structures in society. It is an act of love to respond to the needs of our neighbours and, as the *Compendium* says, "it is an equally indispensable act of love to strive to *organise and structure society* so that one's neighbour will not find himself in poverty".(50)

"There are many times when I grow impatient at the luxury of the Church, the building programs, the cost of the diocesan school system, and the conservatism of the hierarchy. But then I think of our priests. What would we do without them? They are so vital a part of our lives, standing by us as they do at birth, marriage, sickness, and death – at all the great and critical moments of our existence – but also daily bringing us the bread of life, Our Lord Himself, to nourish us. 'To whom else shall we go?' we say with St. Peter."

Dorothy Day(51)

"Father, you have given all peoples one common origin, and your will is to gather them as one family in yourself. Fill the hearts of all with the fire of your love, and the desire to ensure justice for all their brothers and sisters. By sharing the good things you give us, may we secure justice and equality for every human being, an end to all division and a human society built on love and peace."

Collect of the Mass "For the Development of Peoples", 1975(52)

SEE

What do you see in the church, your own parish, diocese, the national or international church? What gives you hope, what troubles you?

Where do you see the church in your context? Is it on or at the margins of society? Can it see the world from the point of view of the margins? Does it accompany those on the margins?

Do you know your local community, your own parish? Who are the isolated ones, the vulnerable ones? Who has just lost a job, or is struggling with child care? What are the prevailing attitudes in the parish? Is there any unacknowledged racism, sexism, or class attitude?

Do you know the local community beyond the parish? Where is the disadvantage, the isolation, the injustice, the fear of violence and intimidation? Where is the Spirit at work in people of goodwill?

Of the current work in the parish, what looks like the building up of the kingdom of God? What looks like a distraction, or a giving in to temptation?

DISCERN

What does the Gospel and the teaching of the Church tell us about the mission of the Church?

What does that mean for your community in its time and place?

Where do you feel the gentle pull of the Spirit? Is there time for prayer, for dialogue, for listening?

ACT

What might be done to make the church in your context truer to its mission and who might be best placed to do it?

How might the church in your context engage more with the local community, to enter more deeply into the work of social justice, tackling the causes of poverty, restoring dignity?

Sanctifying God,
Spirit who hovered over
the chaos of the waters in the beginning,
who inspired the prophets of justice,
who overshadowed Mary, Mother of God,
ark of the covenant;
Spirit who breathed peace into the upper room of fear,
Spirit burning in the heart of the Church
at Pentecost:

give us the grace
to see what is hidden in plain sight,
to know what must be done
to build up the kingdom of love, peace and justice;
flood our hearts with love,
make us holy in your sight,
let us enter into the joy
of the new creation.

Chapter THREE References

1. Second Vatican Council, *Lumen Gentium* (Dogmatic Constitution on the Church), 1
2. *Lumen Gentium*, 36
3. *Lumen Gentium*, 8
4. *Lumen Gentium*, 8
5. Pope Francis, *Evangelii Gaudium* (The Joy of the Gospel), 198
6. *Lumen Gentium*, 8
7. John Shea, *The Relentless Widow: The Spiritual Wisdom of the Gospels for Christian Preachers and Teachers (Luke, Year C)* (Collegeville: Liturgical Press, 2006), 28
8. *Compendium of the Social Doctrine of the Church* (London: Bloomsbury, 2004), 38
9. Kenneth Bailey, *Jesus Through Middle Eastern Eyes: Cultural Studies in the Gospels* (London: SPCK, 2008), 154
10. *Compendium*, 91
11. *CCC*, 2448
12. *Lumen Gentium*, 31
13. Pope Paul VI, *Octogesima Adveniens*, 48
14. *Compendium*, 52
15. Pope St John Paul II, *Redemptoris Missio* (On the permanent validity of the Church's missionary mandate), 14
16. Pope Leo XIII, *Rerum Novarum* (On Capital and Labour), 16
17. Pope Paul VI, *Populorum Progressio* (On the Development of Peoples), 65
18. Second Vatican Council, *Gaudium et Spes* (Pastoral Constitution on the Church in the Modern World), 26
19. *Gaudium et Spes*, 26
20. *Compendium*, 82
21. *Gaudium et Spes*, 26
22. Robert Calderisi, *Earthly Mission: The Catholic Church and World Development* (New Haven: Yale University Press, 2013), 233
23. *Gaudium et Spes*, 26

24. *Gaudium et Spes*, 26
25. *Gaudium et Spes*, 26
26. Pope St John Paul II, *Sollicitudo Rei Socialis* (On Social Concern), 37
27. *Sollicitudo Rei Socialis,* 38
28. *Sollicitudo Rei Socialis*, 38
29. *Sollicitudo Rei Socialis*, 41
30. *Sollicitudo Rei Socialis*, 42
31. *Compendium*, 86
32. *Evangelii Gaudium*, 187
33. *Evangelii Gaudium*, 188
34. *Evangelii Gaudium*, 178
35. *Evangelii Gaudium*, 177
36. *Evangelii Gaudium*, 182
37. Pope Francis, *Fratelli Tutti* (On Fraternity and Social Friendship), 276
38. Robert Calderisi, 207
39. Robert Calderisi, 40
40. Robert Calderisi, 213
41. Pope Benedict XVI, *Deus Caritas Est*, 31
42. *CCC*, 1373
43. *Evangelii Gaudium*, 177
44. *CCC*, 747
45. *CCC*, 768
46. *Evangelii Gaudium*, 20
47. *Deus Caritas Est*, 31
48. *Deus Caritas Est*, 25
49. Benedict XVI, *Spe Salvi*, 4
50. *Compendium*, 208
51. Dorothy Day, *Loaves and Fishes* (New York: Orbis Books, 1963), 126
52. *Sollicitudo Rei Socialis*, 49

Chapter 4

"Change your life..."

the followers of Jesus

Are you a Catholic, or a disciple of Jesus Christ? Most Catholics in my experience, until very recently, have not been comfortable with the language of discipleship, or being a follower of Jesus. Being a Catholic was identity enough. You had a community, you assented to a set of beliefs; there were rituals, devotions, observances, and the promise of heaven if you steered clear of sin. Disciples of Jesus were more to do with other Christian denominations. In recent years, as the Catholic culture many of us were brought up in has disappeared, there has been a renewed emphasis on being an *intentional* Catholic, not somebody who just turns up because their parents did.

In 2012, Sherry A. Weddell published something of a landmark book, *Forming Intentional Disciples: The Path to Knowing and Following Jesus*. It was prompted by a dramatic decline in Catholic practice in America, a phenomenon reflected across the western world. At the time of publication, only thirty per cent of Americans raised Catholic were still practising. Weddell understood that we could no longer rely on Catholic identity by osmosis, the time had come to form intentional disciples and followers of Jesus Christ in the Catholic Church.

Disciples of Jesus in the Catholic Church are those who have been called to change and conversion of life, baptised in the death and resurrection of Jesus Christ, followers of a path of descent and service rather than the glittering but unpredictable path of ascent the world holds before us. It is a counter-cultural path, but followers of this path believe it is the path to life, a path out of futility. In his public ministry, Jesus our Teacher showed us this path. Some followed him, some were curious for a while and then fell away, some were downright hostile, sensing in this teaching a threat to the way they had ordered the world.

Where your treasure is

Matthew's Gospel, like Mark's, introduces the public ministry of Jesus somewhat differently to Luke's emphasis on a prophetic programme. Their account of the baptism of Jesus has an emphasis on the new creation. Both Mark and Matthew have Jesus coming up "from the water" (Matthew 3:16) and then the descent of the Spirit, like a dove. This is *Genesis 1: the sequel.* The waters are the place of chaos and confusion, all that belittles and baffles human beings. Jesus emerges from the depth of this and, like creation itself, is blessed by the Spirit which hovered over the waters in the beginning. Just as God said of creation in Genesis that it was good, so here we have God saying of Jesus coming out of the water, "This is my Son, the Beloved, with whom I am well pleased" (Matthew 3:17). The new Adam has appeared, creation will be renewed, offered a way out of all that binds it down into futility and violence. This is all happening on our level, in a language we can comprehend. This is the path our baptism opens up for us.

After the temptation of Jesus in Matthew's Gospel during which, as in Luke's account, he works through the distortions of his mission as worldly power and physical satisfaction, Jesus begins his public ministry. His first proclamation is "Repent, for the kingdom of heaven has come near" (4:17). Blood has been spilled in the history of Christianity over the meaning of a single word. "Repent" is one of them. In the Vulgate Bible of St Jerome, in Latin, the translation was "do penance" which led to an emphasis on acts of personal mortification. In the Renaissance period, with the translation of the New Testament into Greek by Erasmus in 1516, the emphasis came back to the original Greek *metanoeite,* which means change your mind, or purpose, your inner self, more than do penance for your sins. The keynote of the new creation is *change,* which implies that we are not currently the best versions of ourselves, we've got a way to go to be more like images of God. This proclamation, unlike the calling of the disciples, is not directed at an individual. It's a message for all of humanity. Salvation is universal and integral.

When Jesus looks at the human condition, what does he see? What do we need to change or be rescued *from*? Matthew adds extensive sayings material to the copy of Mark's Gospel he had in front of him. Some of this was drawn from what is called the "Q" source, collections of the sayings and teachings of Jesus distributed among the very early Christian communities. In Matthew, the Sermon on the Mount is the most extensive example. In this body of teaching we get a reverse portrait of the human condition. We're not bad, but far from perfect. It's a picture of human life as we know it. We love our family, sometimes, but hate our enemy; we pray and give alms, but like other people to know about it; we lust in the secrecy of our hearts; we get angry; if we're hurt, we want to get our own back; we hold on to grudges; we worry about things; we have an attachment to treasures on earth. God looks lovingly on this flawed creature, this mixed blessing; in Jesus, God looked lovingly upon us with human eyes.

The Lord looks on the heart, as we saw in Chapter 1. Jesus looks further into the workings of the heart when he says, "where your treasure is, there your heart will be also" (Matthew 6:21). In other words, if you want to know the condition of your heart, your spiritual centre, have a look in your treasure box. What do you find there? What is the thing you value above all else, that would upset you most if it was taken away? Is it your money, your property, your looks, your prestigious role in society? Jesus says that if that's the case we're looking for happiness in the wrong place. The human being who is free stores up a different kind of treasure. Jesus often taught in parables, but sometimes he got straight to the point, for the avoidance of doubt, as when he said: "You cannot serve God and wealth" (Matthew 6:24). He also says we shouldn't worry about what we're going to eat and wear. This has always seemed a bit harsh to me, because there are people who do worry about what they're going to eat because they're hungry. Jesus is not dismissing this kind of need, but saying don't get caught up in cycles of anxiety that don't leave room for faith. When the physical and social monopolise our consciousness, it will cause anxiety. Faith in God is the true treasure.

One of the most memorable portraits of an alienated human being in the Gospels is offered by Luke. When Jesus is goaded by someone in the crowd to sort out his inheritance for him, Jesus warns him that "one's life does not consist in the abundance of possessions" (Luke 12:15). To make the point vivid, he tells the story of the rich man whose land produced abundantly. This was the gift of the Creator, but he didn't see it that way. To him, it was his private gain. He builds bigger barns to hoard his wealth. He has no conception of the universal destination of goods. He is content, it seems, but he is remarkably alone. He literally talks to himself, "Soul, you have ample goods laid up for many years; relax, eat, drink, be merry" (Luke 12:19). This image of accumulated wealth and pleasure is uncomfortably close to home. It's interesting that God doesn't condemn the man (as we've noted already, there is no condemnation in God), but he calls him a fool. He's spent his life accumulating the wrong kind of treasure. The irony is that while the man thinks he is living life to the full – as a self who has gathered in the fruits of creation – he is in fact a depleted self, alone, empty of the life of God.

In the beatitudes, at the beginning of Matthew's Sermon on the Mount, another kind of human being is depicted: the one who is "blessed", or close to God. This person is poor in spirit, knowing their need for God; a mourner who feels the pain of loss because they have loved; they are meek, not seeking to dominate others; they are merciful, pure in heart, not run by the desire to manipulate and get their own way; they are peacemakers, determined to do what they can to put an end to conflict; they are persecuted because they pursue justice, right relations and a distribution of the goods of the earth that God would approve of; they will be reviled because by their very loving existence they undermine so much of what the world needs to function. This is the person specification of the follower of Jesus, one who has changed, who has woken up and lives in a different consciousness in the kingdom of God; one who was lost, but now is found, was blind but now can see. This is the Christian vision of human flourishing, quite different to the wisdom of the world at that time; indeed it is a vision which is still at odds with what the world regards as human flourishing today.

Put away your old self

What Jesus calls for is change from one state to another, a progressive change, a journey over a lifetime, a process of growing up spiritually. The Council of Trent (1545-1563) talked about this as a "translation" from being a child of the first Adam, with all its delusions and wrong attachments, "to the state of grace and the adoption of the sons of God through the second Adam, Jesus Christ".[1] It goes on to talk about being born again in baptism. The section on justification makes it clear that this is not something we can achieve through any merit on our part. It is the predisposing grace of God which prompts us towards right relations. God "touches the heart"[2] but we need to co-operate. It is by our faith, the trust of an open heart, that we can be transformed by grace. What is so striking about the way God treats his creatures is the lack of coercion. God is not a bully. God is not frightening. It took us a long time to work that out, but it was clear in the upper room in Jerusalem, in the final theophany of the divine, when the risen Jesus appeared with words of peace.

This "translation" from one state to another we refer to as formation, or being formed, transformed from one state to another which looks more like Christ. The scriptural inspiration for the concept of spiritual formation is found in St Paul's letter to the Galatians, one of the earliest books of the New Testament, written perhaps only twenty years after the death and resurrection of Jesus. It is extraordinary how much Christian understanding developed in those few years, inspired by the Holy Spirit. Paul writes to his converts, "My little children, for whom I am again in the pain of childbirth until Christ is formed in you" (Galatians 4:19). Paul uses the word *morphoo* for form, which is close to *metamorphoo*, from which we have metamorphosis. It refers not just to an outer change, but more importantly to a change of essential nature.

In another part of the same letter, Paul uses the image of being crucified with Christ. He identifies so closely with Christ that he can say "it is no longer I who live, but it is Christ who lives in me" (Galatians 2:20). This makes us more fully human, the images of God we were meant to be. It's an indwelling, a kind of divine possession, not one that displaces or dominates us, but rather an indwelling that sets us free. It is not a language the world wants to hear. The self-defining individual of our secular world only sees possession negatively, as in being possessed by rage, or evil, or addiction. But this is precisely what formation involves for the Christian, being "possessed" or indwelt by God in a way that does not displace us, that is not controlling or terrifying, but that nourishes our vocation on this earth, which is to love.

In his letter to the Ephesians, St Paul refers to a kind of before and after of discipleship. He talks about putting away "your old self, corrupt and deluded by its lusts" (Ephesians 4:22). This is the "old Adam", the life of what we've called original sin, the life of falling short, of missing the mark. St Paul invites his community to "be renewed in the spirit of your minds, and to clothe yourself with the new self, created according to the likeness of God in true righteousness and holiness" (Ephesians 4:23-24). This is the transformation of discipleship, a journey from an old to a new self, one which is much more a likeness of God, a way of being which is "approved" by God. A transformation which we do not earn, but which is a gift, made possible only by God's grace, through faith.

The Christian tradition has developed the "stages" on the path of transformation. There are generally three, sometimes four. The classic "three ways" of spiritual transformation are purgation, illumination and union. The purgative way is usually related to some sort of "awakening", when we realise that our way of life is not life-enhancing and a bigger vision of life opens up in the encounter with the forgiveness of God. We see the emotion this can generate in a number of scenes in the Gospel. For example, the woman who gate-crashes the dinner party at the house of

Simon the Pharisee because she heard that Jesus was there. Jesus had been embarrassed by his host by not being offered any of the usual courtesies extended to a guest – washing of feet, a kiss, anointing of the head – but the woman has washed the feet of Jesus with tears. Why? She has encountered God's forgiveness in Jesus, she has been "loosed" from her attachment to a self-destructive lifestyle. Therefore, "she has shown great love" (Luke 7:47). We'll look at this beautiful passage in more detail in Chapter 8.

This awakening leads to "purgation", which is a kind of long cleaning-out of our hearts, our lifestyles, even our subconscious. It is in this process that we let the Spirit of God in to dwell in us, to work in us, revealing the aspects of our "old life" that need to be changed. This is when we are in the "how" of discipleship, developing those practices (see: Part II) which will help the purgative process. There are layers of psychology here I am not qualified to deal with. There are many reasons, hidden in childhood, for why we turn out the way we do with our needs for security, pleasure or possessions which run our normal lives. There are also aspects of personality which are a "given" of genetics which may be harder to purge but we trust in the Spirit to change us, slowly, over time. There are some people, like St Paul, who have the "road to Damascus" experience and receive the full "download" of revelation in a 24-hour period. For most, the process of purgation and transformation is slow, seen in little gains. It might even just look like being a bit kinder at home, a bit less likely to take offence, quicker to laugh, slower to condemn, more attentive to the people around me, beginning to be aware of those in my community who are disadvantaged and how I might become engaged.

The second and third stages are "illumination" and "union". Illumination is when we've come to depend on God rather than our own capacity. We experience God within and have handed control of the relationship over to God. It's as if we gave God the hitchhiker a lift and now find that he is the driver, with no fear in that arrangement at all. Mark A. Maddix comments that "illumination is characterised by increasing social concerns – not out of obligations but out of a deep sense of God's love for others".[3] If it is the love of God which dwells in our hearts then we know that by its fruits, which St Paul describes as, "Love, joy, peace, patience, kindness, generosity, faithfulness, gentleness, and self-control" (Galatians 5:22). It is not love unless it is shared and seeks the good of others. Living for others becomes more characteristic of our life. The *Compendium* puts this strongly when it says that conversion of heart "imposes the obligation" of bringing remedies to institutions and living conditions when they do not conform to the norms of justice. This obligation becomes "a firm and constant determination to work for the good of all people and of each person, because we are all really responsible for everyone".[4]

The final stage of "union" or the "unitive way" we normally associate with the mystics, and by mystics I don't just mean the saints, but those everyday mystics we may have had the pleasure to meet. This is characterised as complete oneness with God in which we find ourselves "caught up in adoration, praise, and a deep peace that passes all understanding".[5] We may have had glimpses of this profound sense of oneness, perhaps in prayer, or in a relationship, at the birth of a child, in nature, in the experience of art, but for most of us it is only a glimpse, not a state we inhabit permanently. When you meet someone who does live in that state, what is so striking is the deep peace they exude, their remarkable attentiveness to the person in front of them; someone who is a friend of God, and dwells in his house.

It seems that this change we are called to involves a kind of dying to self, the old self or ego, and a coming alive in the life of the Spirit as a "new creature"(6) who, as St Paul says, "walk[s] in newness of life" (Romans 6:4), seeing the world with the compassionate eyes of Christ because the love of Christ lives in us. This love, like any virtue, grows by being habitual. It does not reside in the head, although the head has an understanding of it. It lives in our hearts and is enacted in our lives. For me, the most compelling examples of this change in people are to be found in the Gospels. There we see the human drama of discipleship, people a bit like us trying to respond to Jesus, trying to change, but facing confusion, set-backs, doubts, and then, in time, coming to the maturity of the "mind of Christ" (Philippians 2:5).

They followed him

At the beginning of his ministry, after he had proclaimed the need for change, Jesus called his disciples. We shouldn't rush past that very familiar point. Jesus needed the help of human beings to carry out the project of the new creation, just like God needed the help of Adam and Eve to till and keep the garden. As we noticed in Chapter 2 at the beginning of John's Gospel, the call is passed on from person to person, but not imposed. It's a choice to turn away from the world and its ways and grow into a new way of being and belonging. It's not a career path, it's not an ascent. It's more like downward mobility, following the path of a God who "emptied himself" (Philippians 2:7). This is not, as we've said before, degradation. It is freedom, the freedom of the children of God. This new kingdom needs disciples, students of a new way of being in the world, and ambassadors who will spread the word, by witness and example. Disciples in *community*, who learn from each other and support each other on the way. The project gets under way on the shores of the lake of Galilee, on the margins of a small country on the margins of the Roman Empire. The ones who are called to be its agents are not the powerful, the intellectual or moral elite, but workers, fishermen.

Gerhard Lohfink observes that at the time of Jesus, there was a model of discipleship, of being a student, which involved the study of the Torah with a rabbi. In this case, students sought out the teacher, never the other way round. Lohfink says, "there is not a single story in the rabbinic tradition in which a rabbi called a student to follow him".[7] The student sought out the teacher, but was not known as one who followed the teacher. The formula for this arrangement was always expressed as the student studying Torah with a particular rabbi, not that the student was following the rabbi. In Mark's Gospel we see a remarkable turnaround of this tradition. On the shores of the lake of Galilee, Jesus said to Simon and his brother Andrew, "Follow me and I will make you fish for people" (Mark 1:17). As with everything in Mark, the response is immediate, there is an urgency to all this: "And immediately they left their nets and followed him" (Mark 1:18). If we place the emphasis on *him*, we can hear how radically different this kind of discipleship was. They followed Jesus. This was about personal attraction. They sensed something here that was bigger than them, something of the will of God. Why else would you leave your family and your occupation for a carpenter from Nazareth?

In the rabbinic tradition, forty-eight things are listed as required for knowledge of the Torah, the law of Moses. As well as study, listening, purity of heart and so on, there is something called "serving the wise". The student would live with his rabbi (the stable location was important) and perform the functions of a servant: washing the master's feet, serving at table, cleaning out the courtyard. The point was not to demean the student but for them to spend time with the master, to observe closely how he lived the Torah. What Jesus proposed was unheard of: "the Son of Man came not to be served but to serve" (Mark 10:45). For Jesus the priority for his disciples was not the study of the Torah, but a new way of being together. He does not allow himself to be served; he is the servant; it is he who washes their feet.

As Lohfink observes, "Under the sign of the now-inbreaking reign of God, human community must also be renewed – finally to become what the Torah had always intended it to be."[8] Jesus did not set up a school, or house of study. He invited his disciples to follow him onto the highways and byways of the human experience, living precariously, encountering the full range of human need, healing the sick, exorcising demons, restoring the outcast to the community. What we might call an "immersion experience" in the human condition. Within this formation on the road "there took place a daily exercise, a daily inculcation of the new community of discipleship – involving for example, the rule that disciples had to forgive one another seventy-seven times a day" (Matthew 18:21-22).[9]

Rowan Williams, the former Archbishop of Canterbury, says that being a disciple of Jesus is to be in a state of attentiveness and expectancy. Those who have responded to this call find themselves looking at life very differently, they take on a new identity, symbolised by the re-naming of some disciples in the Gospel (Peter, for one). Life has a new horizon, they have left behind old certainties and patterns of living to join Jesus on the road, praying for "daily bread" since they literally don't know where the next meal is coming from. This new path in life is portrayed very harshly at times: "Whoever does not carry the cross and follow me cannot be my disciple" (Luke 14:27).

We're being invited to follow a victim to his death, to walk the path of the outcast, the despised one. Williams says that "Being where Jesus is means being in the company of the people whose company Jesus seeks and keeps. Jesus chooses the company of the excluded, the disreputable, the wretched, the self-hating, the poor, the diseased; so that is where you are going to find yourself."[10] If we "abide" in Jesus, if our discipleship is to be what Williams calls "non-intermittent" but a way of being, then we will find ourselves in the same sort of company Jesus is in, since discipleship is "not about choosing our company, but choosing the company of Jesus".[11]

The company of Jesus was quite a collection. As he went along, people joined him, mostly from the margins of society, the ones who were excluded either by illness, disability, moral judgement, or social ostracism. One day, Jesus and his followers were leaving Jericho, on the road to Jerusalem. Bartimaeus, a blind beggar, was sitting by the side of the road. In a spiritual sense, we are all born blind, sitting by the side of the road, unable to make our way to Jerusalem. Bartimaeus heard that Jesus was passing and called out, "Jesus, Son of David, have mercy on me" (Mark 10:47). He is told to be quiet by many of the people around Jesus. This is a crowd dynamic at work again, keeping the excluded one on the margins. They haven't yet fully grasped the compassion of Jesus for human weakness. They are in formation. Bartimaeus is undeterred; he calls out again. There are people in the Church, as we noted already, who get in between us and Jesus, who operate out of their own understanding of what is acceptable and what is not. Jesus shows them how he operates.

He stops and tells the crowd to call Bartimaeus. The same people who were an obstacle have now been encouraged to open up a path to Jesus for others. They are learning too.

They say to Bartimaeus, "Take heart; get up, he is calling you" (Luke 10:49). Now Bartimaeus has a lightness about him. He springs up and comes to Jesus. He is on the verge of new life. A remarkable feature of the way Jesus engages with people is the respect he shows them, the time he takes to speak to them, to examine their motivation. He does not go around like some divine wizard zapping stricken people with his wand. He does not grant every wish, since some of them are not life-enhancing, as when James and John in the previous *pericope* (passage) in Mark's Gospel ask for seats on either side of Jesus "in [his] glory" (10:37). They don't yet understand that the "seats" on either side of Jesus would be occupied by two thieves on crosses outside the city walls.

Jesus says to Bartimaeus, "What do you want me to do for you?" (Mark 10:51). Bartimaeus wants to see, like we all do. Jesus does not draw attention to his own power, the miraculous cure involves no great display. Instead, he draws attention to the faith of Bartimaeus. "Go; your faith has made you well" (Mark 10:52). I often puzzle over that line. What faith did Bartimaeus have? How much could he have known about Jesus and what he represented? As we've seen, it took the closest of the disciples long enough to work all this out. The faith of Bartimaeus was more like the desire of a trusting heart, vulnerability, a step in the dark, literally, to be caught in the embrace of God. Faith is the "gateway" virtue of the disciple, that first step towards the new life of God in Jesus, which is itself a gift, prompted by the Holy Spirit. It will need to grow in understanding of course, in that other definition of faith, as when we say, "the Catholic faith". It will need to be lived out in hope and love. In the Catholic tradition, faith is incomplete without hope and love. This faith is not a personal gain. It allows in the life of God, which is not a private possession, but a dynamic force which reaches out to the needs of the world.

In a moment which I find humorous, Bartimaeus is told to go after he's been cured. Not everybody is called to follow Jesus. But he does the opposite, he "followed him on the way" (Mark 10:52). Since his name was preserved in the oral tradition which was handed on in the early church, Bartimaeus must have been known as one of the group that followed Jesus, all the way to Jerusalem. Once we've come into contact with the healing power of Jesus, a new attachment forms and we want to stay close to this source of new life. This is not the case for everyone in the Gospels, which is what makes the stories so human, so real. The rich young man, for example, is also attracted to Jesus. He seeks him out in the traditional manner of a student looking for a rabbi. But he hasn't quite understood the implications of following *this* rabbi. He can't quite make the full and final commitment, he can't let go of his attachment to wealth, so he goes away sad, but held in the loving gaze of Jesus.

Peter: a journey of faith

Someone else who was there the day Bartimaeus was cured would have been Peter. Maybe he led the chorus of the ones who tried to keep this embarrassingly loud beggar away from Jesus. We don't know, it doesn't say, but we do know that to begin with none of the disciples encouraged Bartimaeus to approach Jesus. I've often taken great comfort from the story of Peter in the Gospels. His journey of discipleship strikes me as being very human, very reassuring. He's got a big heart, he's impulsive. He must have been fit and agile, like all the fishermen on the lake of Galilee. He was married, as suggested by Jesus' cure of his mother-in-law. We don't know if he had children. But one day, when he was cleaning his nets on the shore of the lake, minding his own business, Jesus came along and stepped into his boat. His life would never be the same again.

In a phrase which challenges everybody who'd rather have a comfortable life, Jesus said to Peter, "Put out into the deep" (Luke 5:4). When they haul in the miraculous catch of fish, Peter knows that something life-changing is happening and it scares him. His response is the same as most people's in the Bible when they're called by God: please find somebody else. "Go away from me, Lord, for I am a sinful man" (Luke 5:8). Jesus says what God always says to scared humans, "Do not be afraid" (Luke 5:10). It's a good message for everybody in the Church, whether in a leadership role or not. Do not be afraid, you will not be overwhelmed. Then they "left everything and followed him" (Luke 5:11). I do find that difficult on a practical level. What about Peter's wife, those that depended on his income from fishing? The Gospel is silent on that. Not everything is explained to us.

Throughout their time with Jesus, especially as reported in the synoptic Gospels, Peter and the apostles don't always get the point of what is going on. Their formation is slow, under the guidance of Jesus himself, so we should certainly never despair. Right at the end of Jesus' ministry, at the Last Supper in Luke's Gospel, after all that time with Jesus, all that learning how to be disciples, when his enemies are circling, when Jesus is giving his very self to them in bread and wine as a memorial, what are they arguing about? *Who is the greatest?* They're still in rivalry, still in the "old Adam", not "changed" into missionary disciples. Jesus had such patience with them, indeed *has* patience, with all stumbling disciples. Not for the first time, Jesus delivered a lesson on what being a disciple looks like. They are not to lord it over anybody but to be "like one who serves" (Luke 22:26), since Jesus was among them "as one who serves" (Luke 22:27).

This was a revolution in thought and practice. No wonder it took a long time to sink in. In the ancient world, those who served were looked down on; in Rome the guests at supper would wipe their greasy hands on the hair of the servants. Those who "ruled it over" others were the successful ones, the powerful ones, worthy of honour. That is not the way of the kingdom of God.

Things go from bad to worse for Peter at the Last Supper. Jesus tells him that he will be sifted, like wheat, shaken up to separate what is good from what is chaff. Jesus lets Peter know that he will fail but he will come back and strengthen everybody else. Peter the impulsive is having none of this talk. "Lord, I am ready to go with you to prison and to death!" (Luke 22:33). But alas not yet. That same day, Jesus would be a prisoner and be put to death. There is no record in the tradition of Peter at the crucifixion. He does follow Jesus after his arrest and warms himself by the fire in the courtyard. A servant girl stared at him. This is the stare of accusation, the stare that spreads through the crowd and fixes people in places of separation in order to scapegoat and shame them. She says, addressing the others, "This man also was with him" (Luke 22:56). Peter denies this. Three times in total he denies knowing Jesus and on the third denial, on the cockcrow, "The Lord turned and looked at Peter" (Luke 22:61). This is Luke the master storyteller at his finest. He would've been a superb film director. The look of Jesus should not be seen as a look of reproach. Earlier, Jesus had said that he would pray for Peter. It is an extraordinary moment of loving connection in the midst of trial and turmoil. Disciples may fail, Jesus holds us in a loving gaze nevertheless.

In John's Gospel, after the Resurrection, Jesus appears to his disciples on the shore of the lake. Just as Peter denied Jesus three times on the eve of his death, so now he is given three opportunities to know he is forgiven. Jesus asks him, "Simon son of John, do you love me more than these?" (John 21:15). The Greek word for love which Jesus uses is *agape*. The Christian community soon abandoned all the other Greek words used for love – *eros, storge, phileo* – and settled on *agape* – a word for a new understanding of love that needed to apply not just to our family, our neighbour, but to all the world, even our enemy. This wasn't just a feeling, this was a deliberate policy of life involving head, heart and hands. This was the kind of love Jesus had shown all the way to the cross.

Peter answers Jesus, "Yes Lord; you know that I love you" (John 21:15), but Peter uses the word *phileo* for love, which is more like affectionate friendship, to cherish someone, not quite the *agape* Jesus was asking for. Jesus asks again, "Peter, do you *agape* me?" Again, Peter replies, "Lord, you know that I *phileo* you." Then very movingly, when Jesus asks Peter a third time, to finally erase the third denial, he says to him, "Simon son of John, do you *phileo* me?" It's as if Jesus acknowledges that right now that's the best that Peter can offer, but he is on a journey which will end in martyrdom, when Peter finally shows *agape* for his Lord. But it will take time, the journey of a lifetime. When Peter's all too human love for the Lord has been established, then he is confirmed in his leadership role, which is pastoral. "Feed my sheep" (John 21:17).

Raymond E Brown, the renowned Catholic scripture scholar, has pointed out in his study of John's Gospel, "the consistent and deliberate contrast between Peter and the Beloved Disciple, the hero of the Johannine community".[12] In five of the six scenes where the Beloved Disciple is mentioned, he is explicitly contrasted to Peter. At the Last Supper, he leans on the chest of Jesus, while Peter signals to him for information (John 13:23-26); after the arrest of Jesus, he accompanies him into the high priest's palace, while Peter waits outside and denies Jesus; he is at the foot of the cross with Mary, while Peter has disappeared; on the morning of the Resurrection, he outruns Peter to the tomb and "saw and believed" (John 20:8), as opposed to Peter who only saw the linen cloths. In the post-resurrection scene of Peter's rehabilitation which we have just looked at, it is the Beloved Disciple who recognises Jesus standing on the shore and tells Peter who it is.

For Brown, this is no accident. The Beloved Disciple embodies the fullness of Christian perception, is closer to Jesus than the representative of the "apostolic" Church. This of course may represent tension between the various Church communities at the time. John is certainly not dismissing apostolic foundation, but according to Brown, "he makes 'disciple' the primary Christian category".(13) Unlike Paul's image for the Church of the body and its members, John's image of the vine and branches places emphasis on one central concern: "dwelling on the vine or inherence in Jesus".(14) Discipleship based on love is the most important thing in John's Gospel, to the extent that Peter's investiture in the role of shepherd is only conveyed after he has answered the question, "Do you love me?" (21:15-17). Even then, Jesus alters the "terms" of the question to meet Peter where he is.

Lumen Gentium, one of the "dogmatic constitutions" of the second Vatican Council, which we looked at earlier, stresses that everybody in the Church shares "in the one priesthood of Christ"(15) and "all are called to holiness"(16). Although there are different ministries in the church, "yet there is a true equality of all with regard to the dignity and action common to all the faithful concerning the building up of the body of Christ".(17) In John's Gospel, there are no words of institution at the Last Supper. There is instead the remarkable scene in which Jesus reveals the nature of God, symbolically represented by taking off his outer robe (John 13:4). He shows his disciples that loving service is at the heart of God, by washing their feet. He says to them, "I have set you an example, that you also should do as I have done to you" (John 13:15).

In a speech to commemorate the fiftieth anniversary of the institution of the synod of bishops, Pope Francis said, "Jesus founded the Church by setting at her head the Apostolic College, in which the Apostle Peter is the 'rock' (cf. Matthew 16:18), the one who must confirm his brethren in the faith (cf. Luke 22:32)."(18) He went on to say that the Church is an inverted pyramid and the top is found at the base: "It is in serving the people of God that each bishop becomes, for that portion of the flock entrusted to him, *vicarius Christi*, the vicar of that Jesus who at the Last Supper bent down to wash the feet of the Apostles (cf. John 13:1-15). And in a similar perspective, the Successor of Peter is nothing else if not the *servus servorum Dei*." The Pope is the symbol of unity in the Church, the head of the college of bishops and, following the example of our self-emptying Lord, a servant. The Church does not regard power and authority as the world does. In the same speech, Pope Francis said, "For the disciples of Jesus, yesterday, today and always, the only authority is the authority of service, the only power is the power of the cross."

Priority of adult formation

Being a disciple is the journey of a lifetime, a journey of change and growth, in faith, evident in virtue and good works. The journey for most of us is slow, undramatic, in real time. There may be some "mountain top" moments, but mostly we're on the plain of the everyday. And the everyday dimension of discipleship is key. Being a disciple of Jesus is not a Sunday habit. It doesn't just mean calling yourself a Catholic, believing in certain things, and then in every other respect being much like everybody else in society. As Rowan Williams said, it's a "non-intermittent" state, a way of being and belonging. It's not a solo project. It takes place in the community of the Church, hopefully with the accompaniment of a friend or guide, but that alas is not guaranteed. Being formed in a community, we are accountable to that community, less likely to head off down cul-de-sacs, more likely to be carried when our own resources are exhausted. Or so it should be. It's not easy either. It needs work on our part, daily work, a daily walk of trust, to become more like Christ. It is a path of gradual detachment from the obsession with physical, social and financial preoccupations; gradual release from the calculations and manipulations of the ego. It is a path of growing in grace, in self-giving love, a formation, indeed a reformation, of the heart.

The Church offers the Lord's disciples abundant resources to nourish them on the journey, to sustain the formation of the heart. In 1999, the bishops of England and Wales published a document entitled, *The Priority of Adult Formation*. The document stresses that formation, or formation for mission, is a lifelong project. It should be a systematic and comprehensive exposition of the faith to help disciples grow in knowledge of the faith and how faith should be enacted in the world today, "affirming what is good but also pointing out what is harmful and contrary to the gospel". It should be an integrated and coherent approach which revolves around four dimensions of faith, "to be known, celebrated, lived and translated into prayer". This is inspired by the manner in which Jesus formed his disciples, "Formation in doctrine and scripture, liturgy, the commitment to justice and discipleship, and prayer".(19)

The document affirms that faith involves "a change of life, a metanoia". This conversion arises from the heart, "from the depth of the human person". One interesting statement in the document, quoting the Vatican's *General Directory for Catechesis* (1997), is a call for an emphasis on "the social teaching of the church, human rights and a preferential option for the poor".[20] The *Directory* acknowledges that "too little emphasis has been given in the past to social doctrine". In Part II, we will look in more detail at the four dimensions of faith: scripture, liturgy, prayer and commitment to justice. This is the *how* of our faith: the resources and practices that will nourish and sustain us on the journey to be more like Christ, for our sake and for the sake of the world. In these first four chapters we have looked at the *why* of our faith which is that God loves us, loves creation, is for us, is with us in his Word made flesh, is in us in his transforming Spirit, and calls us out of our old way of being to a new and unimaginably richer existence, a life of compassion and service.

"I am a mission on this earth; that is the reason why I am here in this world. We have to regard ourselves as sealed, even branded, by this mission of bringing light, blessing, enlivening, raising up, healing and freeing. All around us we begin to see nurses with soul, teachers with soul, politicians with soul, people who have chosen deep down to be with others and for others."

Pope Francis[21]

For personal reflection

SEE

Where do you see disciples of Jesus today?

Which disciples of Jesus in history – saints or otherwise – do you find most inspiring and why?

When do you most often sense the company of Jesus?

Do you see yourself as a disciple of Jesus? How would Jesus describe your discipleship? Which character in the Gospels do you think you're closest to?

DISCERN

How do the Gospels speak to you about discipleship?

What might be lacking in your own discipleship? What are you holding back?

ACT

What steps might you take to grow as a disciple on the journey to *agape*, to being a saint, to "leaving everything" and following Jesus?

In the next section we'll look at the "how" of being a disciple and some resources and practices which might help you.

Chapter FOUR References

1. *The Canons and Decrees of the Council of Trent* (Charlotte: Tan Books, 1978), 31
2. *Council of Trent*, 31
3. James R. Estep and Jonathan H. Kim, *Christian Formation: Integrating Theology and Human Development* (Nashville: B&H Publishing, 2010), 254
4. *Compendium*, 43
5. *Christian Formation*, 254
6. *CCC*, 1265
7. Gerhard Lohfink, *Jesus of Nazareth: What He Wanted, Who He Was* (Collegeville: Liturgical Press, 2012), 74
8. Lohfink, 75
9. Lohfink, 76
10. Rowan Williams, *Being Disciples: Essentials of the Christian Life* (London: SPCK, 2016), 11
11. Williams, 11
12. Raymond E. Brown, *The Community of the Beloved Disciple* (New York: Paulist Press, 1979), 82
13. Brown, 86
14. Brown, 87
15. *Lumen Gentium*, 10
16. *Lumen Gentium*, 32
17. *Lumen Gentium*, 32
18. Pope Francis, <http://www.vatican.va/content/francesco/en/speeches/2015/october/documents/papa-trancesco_20151017_50-anniversario-sinodo.html>, accessed 23 May 2021
19. Bishops' Conference of England and Wales, *The Priority of Adult Formation* (1999), <https://cbcew.org.uk/plain/wp-content/uploads/sites/3/2018/11/priority-adult-formation-2000.pdf>, accessed 18 August 2021
20. *The Priority of Adult Formation*
21. *Evangelii Gaudium*, 273

PART II
HOW?

"Teacher... what must I do to inherit eternal life?"

Luke 10:25

Chapter 5

Sacred Scripture, "the word of God"

Rome, 1962, 14 November. More than two thousand bishops from all over the world are assembled for the Second Vatican Council, facing each other in row upon row on the bleachers or temporary seating stands erected inside St Peter's Basilica. The business of the session that day was the document on revelation (which would later be known as *Dei Verbum*). Cardinal Alfred Ottaviani introduced the text, which had been prepared in draft by a commission. As soon as he had finished, Cardinal Achille Liénart of Lille took the microphone and declared the text "unacceptable". The motion was seconded and then according to Edward Hahnenberg, the dam broke "and a flood of criticism poured out, causing a crisis not only for the document on revelation but also for the Council as a whole".(1) So just what was the problem with this document and what was at stake?

Opposition to the draft document had already been building, led by the *periti* or theological advisers to the Council, including Karl Rahner and Joseph Ratzinger (who would later become Pope Benedict XVI). They thought it was too caught up in Counter-Reformation polemics, traditional, defensive and anti-ecumenical, rooted in a fortress Church mentality which was hostile to modernity. At the time of the Reformation in the sixteenth century, Martin Luther emphasised "scripture alone", so the Catholic Church responded by defending tradition. The aim was to protect what had come under fire in the Reformation:

Catholic doctrine, sacramental practice and Church structure. The draft document was very much in that mode, emphasising *two* sources of revelation: scripture and tradition. Divine revelation was seen as a series of propositions which the Church handed down to the faithful. It also argued that scripture was without error in all things "religious and profane", which was difficult to maintain in the face of scientific evidence without appearing to be fundamentalist. One translation of scripture, the Latin Vulgate by St Jerome written in the late fourth century, was given pre-eminence.

Cardinal Bea, an influential progressive presence at the Council, reminded everyone of Pope John XXIII's opening address when he said that Vatican II was meant to be a pastoral council, unlike previous councils which condemned heresies as "anathema". It was meant to reach out to other Christians and the world. The draft document on revelation was not written in this spirit. In the end, it was voted down and work began on a comprehensive rewrite. Hahnenberg comments that what was at work here were two different visions: "Is the Church an eternal authority, constantly vigilant, defending purity against errors lurking everywhere? Or is the church a community passing through history, handing on the Good News through its life, worship, and teaching?"[(2)] When the Dogmatic Constitution on Divine Revelation (*Dei Verbum*) was finally approved on 18 November 1965, it represented a landmark in the development of Church thinking. Revelation was portrayed not as a series of propositions to which we give assent, but first and foremost as God's desire to communicate with us, to bring salvation through Christ, to be in a relationship with human beings.

God is with us

The message of salvation, in Christian tradition, is *heard*. St Paul says, "Faith comes from what is heard, and what is heard comes through the word of Christ" (Romans 10:17). The message grows in those who receive it, "so that by hearing the message of salvation the whole world may believe; by believing it may hope; and by hoping it may love".[3] Sometimes it seemed as if what we heard was the thunder of Mt Sinai, an angry God, an unstable divine presence that needed to be placated. The hellfire and brimstone image of God which may have prevailed before (and sometimes after) Vatican II is brilliantly evoked by James Joyce in *A Portrait of the Artist as a Young Man*. "The fire of hell is of another quality and was created by God to torture and punish the unrepentant sinner... the fire of hell has this property that it preserves that which it burns and though it rages with incredible intensity it rages forever."[4] From the *Inferno* of Dante to the pulpit thunder of Joyce's Fr Arnall, the Catholic imagination has been haunted – perhaps terrorised is a more appropriate word – by visions of eternal punishment by a God who seems remote from his incarnation in Jesus of Nazareth. It is one of the reasons why Joyce's protagonist, the young intellectual Stephen Dedalus, leaves behind what he sees as the restrictions of Catholic Ireland to find freedom. There was nothing very attractive about that God. Who would follow a God like that out of anything other than fear? How could there be friendship with such an angry presence?

Dei Verbum provides an image of God which is quite different. Human beings can draw near to God and "share in the divine nature".[5] This God "speaks to men as friends",[6] inviting us into relationship. This is the God made flesh who said to those curious disciples, "Come and see" (John 1:39). I wonder if we really believe this. It almost sounds too simple. God as a friend. Not a friend who might let us down, or walk away, but a constant friend, who wishes us to know we are forgiven, to grow into a new creation, to flourish. A friendship which grows like any other friendship, through time spent together, getting to know each other, enjoying each other's company, being there for each other, growing in trust and love for each other. Such a friendship would be difficult between a creator and a creature. Moses is called a friend of God, (Exodus 33:11) but that seemed to be a special relationship, almost representative, not extended to the whole people. Friendship with God as an invitation to the whole human race was confirmed by Jesus when he said, "I do not call you servants any longer... but I have called you friends" (John 15:15).

Jesus is the Word made flesh, "the eternal Word who enlightens all men, so that He might dwell among men and tell them the innermost realities about God".[7] To see Jesus is to see the Father. Everything about him is a communication of the Father: his words and works, but above all his death by crucifixion and resurrection, his forgiveness, his sending the Spirit of truth. We need to hear again and again what he came to say, especially in moments of fear and anxiety: "that God is with us to free us from the darkness of sin and death, and to raise us up to life eternal".[8] God comes looking for us, he always takes the first step, he speaks to us. Our response is faith, a trusting heart, an acceptance of what is good for us. This faith itself is a gift, made possible by God's grace which must "precede and assist".[9] God is before us and with us. The very act of responding in faith is the Spirit within us, "moving the heart and turning it to God".[10] We are not spiritual athletes climbing to God by our own efforts. The best we can do is to cooperate, make room for the Spirit.

Faith grows into hope when we hear what God in Jesus is saying to us. This message comes to us from the apostles, who were entrusted with the good news. Under the guidance of the Holy Spirit they passed on "what they had received from the lips of Christ, from living with Him".[11] The eyewitness nature of the tradition is very important. When the apostles were choosing a replacement for Judas, St Peter was adamant that it had to be someone who was with them "beginning from the baptism of John until the day when he was taken up from us – one of these must become a witness with us to his resurrection" (Acts 1:22). Something happened to those ordinary men and women, something extraordinary. They met the risen Lord, a presence of immense peace, who breathed the Spirit of forgiveness into them. They were *loosed* from their old lives and embarked on a lifelong adventure in a new way of being and belonging in community. They left their lives behind them, their old identities, and committed themselves to being ambassadors of the reign of God. Their testimony is the authority of experience, not the experience of authority.

The preaching of the apostles is what was written down in the Gospels and the writings of the New Testament. The phrase "handed on by the apostles" is very important in the Church. It is this "handing on" that brings people to the faith and helps them live a holy life. This handing on takes place in the family, in the parish, in the school. It takes place by example. When I saw my parents go quiet when we went inside the church and genuflect before we sat down, I learned that we were in a different kind of space where an encounter with the holy was possible. When they taught me prayers at bedtime I learned there was a God – and a guardian angel – looking after me in the darkness. My parents did not introduce me to an angry God. The handing on takes place by teaching, as well as example. In my Catholic primary in Greenock in the late 1960s and early 70s, I learned the basic *catechism* and devotional prayers and was prepared for my first Holy Communion and Confirmation.

Faith needs understanding, it needs to be expressed in words. This deepens faith and in turn enables us to pass on what we believe.

Dei Verbum makes it clear that what is handed on is not preserved under glass, like a fossil: "There is a growth in the understanding of the realities and the words which have been handed down".[12] The Church is on a journey "toward the fullness of divine truth".[13] Scripture and tradition are not two separate sources of revelation. They both flow from "the same divine wellspring".[14] There is only one source of revelation, the eternal Word of God. Scripture is the "word of God"[15] (the small "w" is very important) as set down under the influence of God's Spirit. Tradition preserves and transmits the word of God. In this process "the sacred writings themselves are more profoundly understood",[16] so tradition is our living encounter with the word of God under the guidance of the Holy Spirit. The teaching function of the Church is to authentically interpret the word of God. This is a central feature of Catholicism. Without that teaching function, the danger is that a community fragments along diverse lines of interpretation and practice. This does not undermine the authority of experience, but it helps that experience to find expression within a tradition of generations who have been seized by the same experience and responded in faith.

In the Christian tradition, scripture was regarded as inerrant. This was a puzzle for a modern sceptical mind when faced with stories – like that of Adam and Eve – which historically were unlikely to be accurate. *Dei Verbum* gives us the depth of this teaching. Scripture teaches without error "that truth which God wanted put into the sacred writings for the sake of our salvation".[17] This is not the same as saying that every single line in the Bible is historically accurate. That is self-evidently not the case. But just because it didn't happen doesn't mean it's not true. Since the Enlightenment we've lost the power of the insight that stories can be truth-bearing. Truth is not just everything you can weigh and measure. In sacred scripture truth is presented differently in "prophecy, poetry, or some other type of speech".[18] We are invited to look for the meaning the writer intended in his particular circumstances, in the genre that was being used. The stories of creation that we looked at in Chapter 1 were written as cosmologies, foundation myths which sought to respond to the myths around them with the truth that the world was made by a loving God and was good, that human beings were good, if flawed.

The story of the Good News

The Gospels, according to *Dei Verbum*, have "special pre-eminence"[19] in scripture, because they form the "principal witness"[20] to the life and teaching of the Word made flesh. The Gospels were written in a period of about thirty years, from c. AD 70 to c. AD 100. In 1964, the Pontifical Biblical Commission published *Instruction on the Historical Truths of the Gospel*, a helpful guide to understanding the process by which the Gospels were written. The insights of this document were included in *Dei Verbum*. The document tells us: "To judge properly concerning the reliability of what is transmitted in the Gospels, the interpreter should pay diligent attention to the three stages of tradition by which the doctrine and the life of Jesus have come down to us".[21]

Stage 1: The public ministry of Jesus, from c. AD 30-33. This is what Jesus did and said during his public ministry that was witnessed by his followers. The Commission makes no claim that what we have in the Gospels is an exact record of this time. Most of the life of Jesus, often referred to as the "hidden years", is unknown to us. We know that he lived as an artisan – in Greek a *tekton* (Mark 6:3), a worker in stone and wood – in the small highland village of Nazareth. For the last three years of his life, however, much of what Jesus said and did was known to many people, especially the disciples who followed him from the beginning to the end of his ministry. The way Jesus taught – especially his use of parables and short, memorable sayings, such as "last will be first, and the first will be last" (Matthew 20:16) – helped those witnesses to remember what he said. They also remembered how he made them feel.

Stage 2: The apostolic preaching about Jesus, from c. AD 33-70. This is what the apostles preached about Jesus in the light of his resurrection from the dead. As Denis McBride says, "The earliest preached Gospel began where our written Gospels finish."(22) As a result of their experience of the resurrection, the apostolic preachers came to a fuller understanding of who Jesus was. As we will see when we look more closely at the story of the Road to Emmaus, they came to re-interpret the past and their understanding of Jesus. The early preaching focused above all on the death and resurrection of Jesus and his identity as the incarnate Word. This early focus was necessary since for anyone who listened to these preachers, the biggest stumbling block (literally "scandal") was that the Messiah they preached was crucified as a common criminal, a shameful death. This did not look like the Son of God, but a miserable failure. Then came attention to the deeds and words of Jesus as collections of his parables, sayings and miracles were assembled. As the Christian communities attracted converts and grew in size, there was a need for a more developed catechesis. The teaching and deeds of Jesus were all part of the revelation of the "inner life of God". This growing body of work – oral and probably some written – was not a simple and consistent chronicle of what Jesus did and said. The preachers interpreted the tradition according to the needs of their communities in different contexts, in places like Antioch, Corinth, Ephesus, Rome.

Stage 3: The evangelists' written Gospels, from c. AD 70-100. The stories and sayings which circulated in Stage 2 provided the source material for the four evangelists. Parts of the tradition, especially the passion narratives and collections of sayings, were probably already in written form. What is important to note in this stage is that the evangelists wrote the four Gospels, "selecting some things from the many things which had been handed on by word of mouth or in writing, reducing some of them to a synthesis, explicating some things in view of the situation of their churches".(23) In other words, the evangelists were not setting out to produce historically accurate accounts of the life of Jesus but an account to serve the needs of their own communities. The Commission makes no claim that the evangelists were apostles or eyewitnesses. The scholarly consensus now seems to be that they were not eyewitnesses but heard about Jesus and his ministry from those who were eyewitnesses. This helps to make sense of the differences in the Gospels. If they were all written by eyewitnesses, you would expect more conformity.

The Gospel of Mark was probably the first to be written, somewhere around AD 70, or certainly after the destruction of Jerusalem by the Romans in AD 70 which Mark has Jesus refer to when he says of the Temple, "Not one stone will be left here upon another" (Mark 13:2). Mark's Gospel is distinct in its portrayal of Jesus as the suffering Son of Man, the mystery. The disciples are portrayed as frankly stupid and disloyal. Some have suggested that Mark's Gospel was written in Rome, with Peter as the eyewitness, at a time of persecution for the young Church. Plenty of the scenes could be read that way, for example the storm at sea, when Jesus is asleep in the stern of the boat, apparently unconcerned that the disciples are about to perish. When they rouse him, he chides their lack of faith, "Why are you afraid? Have you still no faith?" (Mark 4:40). He calms the storm and the disciples are filled with awe, as if they had experienced anew the power of their Lord.

Matthew's and Luke's Gospels were written around AD 80. They probably had Mark's Gospel in front of them as well as a common source of written sayings (the "Q" source) and their own material. In Matthew's Gospel we see Jesus as the Teacher of the church, the personification of the Torah who goes up the mountain, like Moses, but to deliver a new law, the law of love, in the Sermon on the Mount. The disciples are smarter than they are in Mark's Gospel, but disloyal. Matthew was in all likelihood writing for a Jewish Christian community. In Luke's Gospel, Jesus is presented as the prophet, who calls people to a programme to reform their lives, warning of the danger of riches. The disciples are the prophetic successors in the life of the Church whose story is continued in "Part 2" of Luke's work, the Acts of the Apostles. In John's Gospel, written perhaps as late as AD 100, Jesus is the man from heaven who performs "signs", who reveals God to his friends, who brings light into the world and is rejected by the world. John's Gospel bears all the signs of a highly polemical atmosphere, as in a courtroom, which reflects the bitter disputes between the Christian and Jewish communities.

All the Gospels have this double focus – on the life and teaching of Jesus, as well as the communities they were written to encourage and inspire. What they all have in common is that they were spiritual sustenance for those communities. In *Dei Verbum* we find a very clear statement that God's word should be revered as much as the Eucharist. What we receive is "the bread of life from the one table of God's word and Christ's body".[24] In the Catholic Church before Vatican II, the scriptures were rarely read by the laity. When my parents went to Mass in the 1930s, 40s and 50s, it was all in Latin. The emphasis was on the sacrifice of the Mass and the sustenance of the body of Christ. Their spirituality was focused on devotions and observances. Vatican II was a great retrieval of scripture in the Catholic community. Fast forward to the late 1970s and 80s and my father is holding a scripture study group in our council flat in Greenock. Crammed into our living room we had Maureen the teacher, Tommy the shipyard shop steward, Agnes the cleaner, and others, about ten in all: ordinary people with a thirst for God's word. My father left school at the age of fifteen; his scripture study was all self-taught, inspired by the great generation of Catholic scholars whose work was encouraged by the Council, like Raymond E. Brown and Joseph Fitzmeyer. The group lasted for years.

They took to heart the insight of *Dei Verbum* that the study of the "sacred page" was "the soul of sacred theology".[25] The lay faithful were strongly urged to undertake "frequent study of the scriptures" in order to get to know their Lord, since as St Jerome said, "ignorance of scripture is ignorance of Christ".[26] What is important to remember is that this is not an academic exercise, this is an encounter with the word of God. *Dei Verbum* stresses that "prayer should accompany the reading of sacred Scripture"[27] so that it becomes a dialogue between us and God: we listen to God, we talk to God. The word of God is "living and active" (Hebrews 4:12), it "reads" us, it works on us for our good. The effect of this nourishment is "enlightening minds, strengthening wills and firing hearts with the love of God".[28] When we "hold it fast in an honest and good heart" (Luke 8:15), the seed of the word of God will bear fruit in us. John Cassian, the fifth century monk and student of the Desert

Fathers, wrote of the need for "daily and hourly turning up the ground of our heart with the gospel plough".[29] Our hearts need to be "turned over" by the Gospel, converted, made open to being formed, or reformed, by the transforming word.

What kind of word has the best chance of turning over our hearts? There were many types of writing available to the evangelists, but they settled on one type which has always spoken powerfully to human beings: the story. The Gospels are narratives, they tell the story of Jesus and his followers. Stories are about human beings in time, in community: their relationships, status, choices, doubts, failures, causes, betrayals, faithfulness. Stories are memorable, interesting, compelling. Stories have a wider reach than esoteric sayings or teaching tracts only accessible to an educated elite. It seems entirely consistent with the God we are talking about in these pages that the means of communication chosen to reach people would be stories which could be remembered and passed on and then written down. God wanted to touch our hearts, to stretch our imaginations, to teach us his kindness by "adapting His language with thoughtful concern for our weak human nature".[30] The good news of God has been handed on to generations of Christians in stories that have comforted and challenged, inspired and provoked, converted and confounded.

Within the story of the Gospels we find another use of story. Jesus revealed the inner nature of God in what he said and in what he did; in who he was. The method of teaching adopted by Jesus, the pedagogy of God, if you like, was primarily the parable. In Mark's Gospel we hear that "he did not speak to them except in parables" (4:34), although the disciples had their own private seminars later on. Jesus' use of parables was not an innovation. Parables were a widely used form at the time, and we find them in the Old Testament. What was striking was the number of parables told by Jesus. There are around forty parables in the synoptic Gospels. The content is also striking. These were not stories to entertain, or to deliver a nugget of wisdom, or to reassure people that their worldview was the right one. Jesus did not end up dead because he told harmless spiritual stories to make people feel better. As Denis McBride says, "he told dangerous stories which radically challenged what was happening in the real kingdoms of his own time".[31]

We've noted already that the keynote of the Galilean ministry was a call to change, to change your mind, your outlook. McBride observes that "the parables are at the service of that radical summons, to question what we take for granted by calling us to change our minds".[32] In the parables, Jesus works on the imagination of his hearers to see the world differently. He looks in particular at vulnerable individuals and oppressive attitudes: a neglected beggar at a rich man's gate, a poor widow, a terrified servant, a destitute son, a stranger beaten up and left for dead on the roadside. He does not provide any comfort for the elite who benefit from oppressive or exploitative social relations. The parable that begins, "There was once a rich man…" is not going to end with any comfort for the rich man. Parables subvert the world by exposing oppression, refusing to acquiesce in the status quo. They break down social divisions between clean and unclean, insider and outsider. Parables offer a reversal of values. In the Reflection following Chapter 8, we'll have a close look at one of the most famous of all Jesus' parables, The Good Samaritan.

Lectio Divina - holy reading

The study of scripture has grown in the Catholic community since Vatican II, with many people taking up *Lectio Divina*, or holy reading of scripture. Fr Thomas Keating, an American Trappist monk, comments on this ancient Christian practice: "Divine reading as the monks conceived it was done not for the sake of information but for insight. It was not to learn something but to encounter Christ".[33] I discovered it about ten years ago, when I had a connection with a local Benedictine monastery. I went to some workshops on Lectio and was hooked. The method, for those who aren't familiar with it, involves an individual or a group approaching a passage of scripture in four stages: *Lectio – Meditatio – Oratio – Contemplatio*. It's common now to add a fifth stage: *Actio*, or *Incarnatio*.

Lectio. Begin your Lectio with a prayer to the Holy Spirit, asking for guidance and discernment. The Spirit we pray to is the same Spirit who was present at the beginning of creation, the same Spirit of peace the risen Jesus breathed on his disciples, the same Spirit under whose influence the inspired works of scripture were written. We invoke this Spirit, asking to be enlightened, strengthened and fired up with love. We then read the passage of scripture slowly. In a group it works well to have different voices reading verses. On your own, writing out the passage by hand is a good way to take it in, as is reading aloud. In the ancient world, people always read "out loud", there was no silent reading. Keating says that the monks of the Middle Ages used to whisper the words so that their bodies were engaged in the conversation. "They would also read very slowly, the whole process of Lectio taking at times a couple of hours."[34] Too much of our reading today is to consume information, clicking from one site to another online. Our attention spans are shrinking. We've lost the ability to read well, read slowly, read prayerfully. This needs to be worked on as a deliberate practice, a central part of the *how* of being a Catholic today.

The Church teaches that there are "senses of scripture". The literal sense, which would be associated with the Lectio stage, is the first sense, but we are encouraged to go beyond that. The document *The Gift of Scripture*, published jointly by the Bishops' Conferences of Scotland, England and Wales in 2005, tells us that "Catholic teaching has treasured the 'spiritual sense' of Scripture, which has been defined as 'the meaning expressed by the biblical texts when read, under the influence of the Holy Spirit'."[35] The spiritual sense of scripture has a number of dimensions which more or less equate to the stages of *Lectio Divina*. A key aspect of the spiritual sense of scripture is that the word of God becomes personal. It is not a historical document. The same Spirit who influenced the human authors influences us today as individuals and as a community gathered around the word of God. Keating says, "It dawns on us that the gospel is about *us*; that our own life is mirrored in its pages."[36] The spiritual sense of scripture is developed in the next stage of *Lectio Divina*.

Meditatio. We allow some silence to let the words settle in our heart. In our busy lives we're not always comfortable with silence. But we need good soil to receive the word of God. An attentive silent heart is good soil. Very often a word or phrase or image will speak to us with particular force. The word of God is personal, it speaks to us. Pope Emeritus Benedict XVI, in his exhortation *Verbum Domini*, said, "The word of God is living and addressed to each of us in the here and now of our lives."[37] What is the scripture saying to me today, in my life? How is God working on my imagination, on my choices, on my determination to change? Some people like to keep a record of their thoughts in a journal. In a group lectio, after a period of silence you can invite people to share a phrase or word that spoke to them. This is known as "echoes", and then the group can move on to share insights and comments, but not as a discussion, or an argument. The insights of others are often very revealing – to hear how the Holy Spirit works through others can teach us things in the passage that we have not noticed.

Oratio. This is our prayer, what we are saying to God, from the depths of our hearts. In a group, people are invited to share their spontaneous prayers if they wish, ending, *Lord, in your mercy*, to which the group replies, *Hear our prayer*. This is affective, or personal prayer, which we'll look at more closely in Chapter 7. Pope Benedict XVI said that "Prayer, as petition, intercession, thanksgiving and praise, is the primary way by which the word of God transforms us."[(38)] When we read the Bible, God speaks to us. When we pray, we speak to God. In the Gospels, Jesus encourages us to speak to God, our loving Father, to name what we need – "Give us this day our daily bread" (Matthew 6:11), "Search, and you will find" (Matthew 7:7). Growth in the Christian life is understanding the difference between what we want and what we need for life in the Spirit. In the Psalms, "the very heart of the Old Testament",[(39)] we see the full range of human emotions expressed in prayer, from rage and even violence, to deep joy and gratitude. God knows what is in our hearts, but he still wants us to be honest with him.

Contemplatio. This is known as "resting in God", not trying to think of anything but maintaining silence, no thoughts, to allow the deeper work of the Spirit to take place. St John of the Cross said that God's first language was silence, all the rest is a poor translation. This is close to what is known as Centering Prayer, which we will look at in more detail in Chapter 7. One of the great obstacles to hearing the word of God is our own agenda and obsessions, what is known in the contemplative tradition as the distractions of the false self. Keating says that the habit of contemplative prayer enables us "to hear the word of God without wax in our ears – that is, to be empty of attachment to our own ideas, programs, and plans".[40] It deepens the process of listening, increases our ability to trust in God. Benedict XVI describes the *Contemplatio* stage of *Lectio Divina* as aiming to create within us "a truly wise and discerning vision of reality, as God sees it, and at forming within us 'the mind of Christ' (1 Corinthians 2:16)".[41] After a suitable length of time the session can be concluded with an Our Father and an invocation to the saint of the day.

Actio. This is associated with the moral sense of scripture, any resolution to act which has been inspired by the word of God, any small steps in the spiritual life I could take, any adjustments to my lifestyle which are overdue, how I might be more attentive to the people I live with, how I might deepen a little my commitment to justice. Keating reminds us of St Augustine's insight into scripture "that we understand more by doing what it says than by how much of it we read".[42] The word of God is generative, it is not like any other text which we might read for information, enlightenment or improvement. In scripture we are encountering God just as much as we encounter God in the Eucharist. When this encounter is part of our daily practice, our daily bread, then we have the possibility of growing in virtue, in faith, hope and love for God, neighbour and creation.

The holy reading of scripture can be undertaken on your own as a daily practice and this will bear much fruit. The Parable of the Sower features in all three of the synoptic Gospels, but it is only in Luke's account that we have "instructions" on how to make sure that the word of God bears fruit. When the word finds the good soil, that soil stands for the ones who, when they hear the word, "hold it fast in an honest and good heart, and bear fruit with patient endurance" (Luke 8:15). We need an open and an honest heart for the word of God to reach us. If we are "choked by the cares and riches and pleasures of life" (Luke

8:14) then the word will not take root. There is no room for the life of God. We are encouraged to "hold it fast", to make it part of our daily life, to persevere in patience, through the periods of doubt and darkness, in the assurance of bearing fruit.

While the Church encourages personal devotion to scripture, there is always an emphasis and preference for community engagement with the word of God. Group Lectio, in my experience, is a profound way to engage with the Holy Spirit teaching us through others. It also forms friendships and bonds of solidarity. More important again, in fact most important, is the prayerful reading of scripture in the liturgy. As Benedict XVI said, "the privileged place for the prayerful reading of sacred scripture is the liturgy, and particularly the Eucharist, in which, as we celebrate the Body and blood of Christ in the sacrament, the word itself is present and at work in our midst".[43] The Eucharist is the primary expression of Church as an interpretive community of the word of God. We hear the Gospels in the context of the whole canon of scripture, juxtaposed with readings from the Old Testament. In the Eucharist we are in the presence of the risen Lord who interprets for us "all the things about himself in all the scriptures" (Luke 24:27), the one who met the two despondent disciples on the road after the resurrection.

The Road to Emmaus: encountering the Word of God

The Road to Emmaus in Luke's Gospel is the story which perhaps best illustrates that the bread of life we receive is from the table both of God's word and of Christ's body. It is also the story that speaks to anybody who has ever walked away from the Church, walked away from the scene of any disaster after we "had hoped" for so much. We all have our own litany of broken dreams. The road to Emmaus is the road of discarded hopes. It's also the road of encounter and turnaround. Let's follow what happens to those two disciples.

First, no one is really sure where Emmaus was. If you go on pilgrimage to the Holy Land today, there are a few places claiming to be the original. Some think it was a Roman spa town, a kind of Las Vegas of the classical world. In that interpretation, these two are on their way to drown their sorrows. It's maybe more helpful to think about where they're coming *from*: Jerusalem. What they're walking away from is the hope which died with the failed messiah hanging on a gibbet outside the city walls. They are talking about what happened, but not agreeing. The Greek word used is *antiballete* (Luke 24:17), which is where we get "ballistic" from. They're throwing it back and forward. In the circumstances, I imagine it could well be a row.

One is called Cleopas, we don't know the name of the other one. Some have speculated that this is Cleopas' wife, who, unlike Cleopas, was at the foot of the cross. This would have made for an interesting *"antiballete" – so where were you then, Cleopas, when we needed you?* Others have suggested that St Luke leaves the identity blank intentionally, as in *N.*, so that for "name" we can insert ourselves in the story. Any disciple might see themselves in this story, walking away from what looked like a disaster, rowing about what it all meant. So let's put ourselves in the story, walking along beside Cleopas, having a row about the Church and what it all means.

Then they are interrupted, which is when the good news starts for them, but they don't get it for a while. They don't "see" properly, they don't recognise Jesus, but they know he's not from "round here" – Cleopas calls him *paroikeis* (24:18), which is stranger, or in the Old Testament, a resident alien. Maybe it was the Galilean accent he heard. Cleopas was closer to the truth than he realised. From the beginning, Jesus was an outsider, with no place "in the inn" (Luke 2:7) and he was executed "outside the city gate" (Hebrews 13:12), which is where we will forever find him, and find ourselves.

With one of the shortest questions in the New Testament – "What things?" (Luke 24:19) – Jesus invites Cleopas and his companion to talk to him, tell him what all this is about. Cleopas shows Jesus just how far off the mark they are, by rehearsing their dashed hopes in the wrong kind of messiah. Even the astounding news that the women have reported an empty tomb did not stop them in their tracks on the road to nowhere. No one is converted by an empty tomb. Jesus is exasperated that they are not getting this; he calls them "slow of heart" (24:25) because they haven't interpreted the prophets correctly. So he helps them. In one of the most famous seminars in history Jesus, our Teacher, takes them through the scriptures to make it clear that the self-emptying path of descent was the route to redemption. If only they had taken notes! Our lives might have been so much easier, but that is not the point here. The point is coming.

At the end of the seminar, as they come near the village, Jesus walked ahead, "as if he were going on" (24:28). In scripture, a theophany (showing of God) happens in passing, as God passed by Moses in the cleft of the rock (Exodus 33:22) and he only saw him from behind. We'll never fully capture this God, he is always in some sense ahead of us, more than us, but never far away. The two disciples utter the sad cry of disciples in every age, "stay with us" (24:29). And that invitation is always answered, God always stays. In fact, as we've said already, it is the Holy Spirit which prompts the cry in the first place: "our desire to thank you is itself your gift", as it says in the Preface of the Mass. It is the cry of faith, and shows the trust and openness which are the prerequisite of being disciples.

So Jesus stays with them and then we have the final part of the revelation, at table, where revelation often happens in Luke's Gospel. Jesus does what he did at the Last Supper, what he did with his life, what his disciples are called to do with their lives: he took, blessed, broke and gave. In that moment of sacrificial giving they recognised him, because that is who he is, that is what he does. Then he is gone, but not gone, since he will forever be present in the Eucharist, in the word, wherever anybody is giving themselves away in love. Now they "see" what being a disciple is all about – the arsonist of the heart has struck. Their hearts, their spiritual centres, are on fire, no longer dimmed and slow. They're on the same page now. They "got up" (24:33), they participate in the resurrection, which for the disciples is participating in the fullness of the Spirit that Jesus revealed.

They turn around from the perennial temptation to walk away, to lose hope, to head off in the wrong direction. They go back to Jerusalem, which is where Jesus was always headed in Luke's Gospel to fulfil his prophetic mission. There we find the Church, the community, the Apostolic A-team, with Peter at the heart of it, the ones who *confirm* that what they're talking about is true, not something dreamt up. And this community is sustained by what the disciples encountered on the road to Emmaus, the word and body of the Lord, given lovingly as food for the life of the world.

HOW

Practical suggestions and resources for growing in faith through the word of God.

The word of God is the bread of life and spiritual bread is best consumed daily, not infrequently. One practice to consider is the daily readings at Mass. You can find these on the Universalis website: https://universalis.com/mass.htm. Or download the Universalis app.

For a daily prayer reflection on the readings of the day, the Jesuit website and app PrayAsYouGo is one of the most popular. There is a 10-15 minute reflection on one of the readings of the day, with beautiful music https://pray-as-you-go.org/. This has been part of my daily practice for a number of years: while walking the dog, driving to work, or doing my "home gym" during lockdown. You'll also find a wealth of other resources from the Jesuit tradition, including a variety of Examen prayers and online retreats.

To find out more about the liturgical calendar and for more information, resources and advice, the Liturgy Office of the Bishops' Conference of England and Wales is recommended: https://www.liturgyoffice.org.uk/

There are many practical guides to *Lectio Divina* and the study of scripture if you want to explore in more depth. A good place to start might be the Bible Society at https://www.biblesociety.org.uk/explore-the-bible/lectio-divina/

There are a number of options for reflections on the Sunday readings, following the three-year liturgical cycle. I would recommend two in particular:

Denis McBride's *Seasons of the Word* (Redemptorist Publications). Reflections on the readings of the full three-year cycle are available in one volume.

John Shea's *The Spiritual Wisdom of the Gospels for Christian Preachers and Teachers* (Liturgical Press). Reflections on the readings of the three-year cycle available in four separate volumes, one for each liturgical year and one for feast days.

In the three-year liturgical cycle of readings, the Gospel of Matthew is the main focus of **Year A**, the Gospel of Mark for **Year B**, and the Gospel of Luke for **Year C**. The Gospel of John features at different times throughout the cycle, especially during Lent and over Easter. To study individual Gospels in more depth, I'd recommend the *Sacra Pagina* series (Liturgical Press), with a separate volume dedicated to each Gospel and other books of the New Testament.

The translation of the Bible that many of us grew up with in the 1970s and 80s was *The Jerusalem Bible*. The principle of this translation was one of *dynamic equivalence*, which sought to render the meaning or intention of the author for a modern audience, rather than a literal translation. This principle has been eclipsed by a more literal approach of *formal equivalence*. This approach informs the translation most commonly used by Catholics, the *New Revised Standard Version* (Catholic Edition).

Chapter FIVE References

1. *Vatican II, The Essential Texts* (New York: Image, 2012), 79
2. *The Essential Texts*, 82
3. Second Vatican Council, *Dei Verbum* (Dogmatic Constitution on Divine Revelation), 1
4. James Joyce, *Portrait of the Artist as a Young Man* (London: Norton Critical Editions, 2007)
5. *Dei Verbum*, 2
6. *Dei Verbum*, 2
7. *Dei Verbum*, 4
8. *Dei Verbum*, 4
9. *Dei Verbum*, 5
10. *Dei Verbum*, 5
11. *Dei Verbum*, 7
12. *Dei Verbum*, 8
13. *Dei Verbum*, 8
14. *Dei Verbum*, 9
15. *Dei Verbum*, 9
16. *Dei Verbum*, 8
17. *Dei Verbum*, 11
18. *Dei Verbum*, 12
19. *Dei Verbum*, 18
20. *Dei Verbum*, 18
21. Pontifical Biblical Commission, *Instruction on the Historical Truth of the Gospels*, VI, 2
22. Denis McBride, C.Ss.R., *Jesus and the Gospels* (Chawton: Redemptorist Publications, 2002), 71
23. *Dei Verbum*, 19
24. *Dei Verbum*, 21
25. *Dei Verbum*, 24
26. *Dei Verbum*, 25
27. *Dei Verbum*, 25

28. *Dei Verbum*, 23
29. John Cassian, *Conferences 1.9* (New Jersey: Paulist Press, 1985)
30. *Dei Verbum*, 13
31. McBride, 29
32. McBride, 24
33. Thomas Keating, *Intimacy with God* (New York: Crossroad, 2015), 95
34. Keating, 96
35. Bishops' Conference of England and Wales, and Bishops' Conference of Scotland, *Gift of Scripture*, 20, <https://www.liturgyoffice.org.uk/Resources/Scripture/GoS.pdf>, accessed 19 August 2021
36. Keating, 97
37. Benedict XVI, *Verbum Domini* (Post-Synodal Exhortation on the Word of God), 87
38. *Verbum Domini*, 87
39. *Gift of Scripture*, 33
40. Keating, 101
41. *Verbum Domini*, 87
42. Keating, 97
43. *Verbum Domini*, 86

The Eucharist,

"a sacrament of love, a sign of unity..."

Compared to the high drama surrounding the passage through Vatican II of *Dei Verbum*, the Constitution on the Sacred Liturgy, *Sacrosanctum Concilium*, had a relatively smooth ride. It was the first text to be debated at the Council, in the autumn of 1962, and was approved overwhelmingly by the bishops on 4 December 1963. The main reason for the relatively uncontroversial passage of this Constitution was that reform of the liturgy had been under way for decades. At the beginning of the twentieth century, a Belgian, Dom Lambert Beauduin, led the way, lamenting the passivity of Catholics at Mass, calling for more active participation. This was supported by the popes, beginning with Pius X (1903-1914), who launched a campaign to encourage Catholics to receive Communion more regularly. Pope Pius XII, in 1947, dedicated an entire encyclical, *Mediator Dei*, to the liturgy. He supported the basic direction of the liturgical reforms which had been gathering pace, especially the call for the active participation of the laity.

The Constitution on the Sacred Liturgy was a milestone in the reform of the liturgy, but was just a beginning. It was more concerned with general principles. The details of reform were entrusted to a commission, called the *Consilium*, which worked under the attentive guidance of Pope Paul VI to restructure the liturgical life of the Church on an unprecedented scale. This is where the impact of Vatican II was felt most keenly by ordinary Catholics. Up until Vatican II, Catholics "attended" Mass (many referred to "hearing" Mass), it wasn't something they participated in. The priest mostly had his back to the people, the language used was Latin, there was a sense of sacred ritual taking place on the altar with little connection to the people in the pews. For many, it was an opportunity for private devotions, like saying the rosary. Missing Mass was a mortal (grave) sin, but that didn't apply if you arrived before the offertory. In other words, the Liturgy of the Word, the reading of sacred scripture, was seen as much less important than the Liturgy of the Eucharist and the Consecration.

By the time I started serving on the altar, around 1970, the priest was facing the people, the Mass was entirely in English, we had modern-sounding hymns and guitars, and we were offering each other a sign of peace (in those days, an awkward nod). For me, as a young boy, the changes had no great significance, since I wasn't really aware of what had gone before. It's only looking back now, having heard the stories of many ordinary Catholics, that I can see that, for some, it was a time of disorientation. A lot of the old certainties seemed to have fallen away. I clearly remember Tommy, our neighbour, who was a shop steward in the shipyards (so detail was important to him), saying to my dad one night at the scripture study group in our house, "But Frank, is it still a mortal sin?" I can't remember what he was talking about (presumably nothing too personal since it was a group discussion) but the plea in his voice brought home to me the reality of a Church in transition, a Church, or at least a laity, that in many ways was growing up. Vatican II was a work of the Holy Spirit, opening up the Church to the modern world, encouraging ordinary Catholics to deepen their faith, for the benefit of building a better world.

We will look more closely in this chapter at some of the main elements of what is known as the *Novus Ordo*, short for *Novus Ordo Missae*, which means the "new order of the Mass". *Novus*

Ordo distinguishes the Mass promulgated by Pope Paul VI in 1969, following the work of the *Consilium*, from the Traditional Latin Mass promulgated by Pope Pius V in 1570. When Pope Paul VI's new Roman Missal (the liturgical book that contains the text of the Mass) was released, it replaced the Traditional Latin Mass which my parents grew up with as the normal form of the Mass in the Catholic Church. The Traditional Latin Mass is still valid, and can be celebrated, but the *Novus Ordo* is the "ordinary" form of the Mass celebrated in Catholic churches. In 2021, Pope Francis issued a decree, *Traditionis Custodes*, which clarified restrictions on the Traditional Latin Mass which, in his judgement, having consulted with the world's bishops, was becoming a source of division in the Church and a symbolic gathering point for those who opposed the reforms of Vatican II.

Sacramental imagination

Before we move on to a brief survey of the elements of the Mass, let's remind ourselves of what we mean by liturgy and in particular the sacraments. The Constitution on the Liturgy is not just about the Mass, but about the liturgy of the Church, "the fountain from which all her power flows".[1] The term liturgy itself derives from the ancient Greek idea of public works, or services. Liturgy is the divine worship of the Church which includes the Mass, the celebration of the sacraments and the Divine Office (the daily prayer of the Church). Through the Church's liturgy we encounter God and we're united with our brothers and sisters in the Church across the world. I've always found it a source of inspiration to think that wherever the sun is rising in the world, somebody, or some community, is saying Lauds, the morning prayer of the Church. In the next chapter, we'll explore in more detail the difference between liturgical prayer and devotional, or affective, prayer, but for now the main point to remember is that the Church's liturgy is her official, public worship.

Catholicism is a sacramental religion. At the heart of our faith is what some have called a sacramental imagination. In *Laudato Si'*, Pope Francis says that "the sacraments are a privileged way in which nature is taken up by God to become a means of mediating supernatural life".(2) He goes on to say that encountering God does not mean fleeing from this world or turning our back on nature. In Chapter 1, we saw some evidence in the liturgy of the Church before Vatican II of a mindset which dismissed the things of the earth. This has been a strong strain in Christianity, the idea that nature is sinful and salvation can only be found by turning our eyes to heaven. This approach forgets the fundamentally *incarnational* reality of the Christian faith, that the Word of God became flesh and, wonderfully, gave himself as food for us, choosing "to reach our intimate depths through a fragment of matter".(3) God does not come to us from heaven, if you like, but from within; "he comes that we might find him in this world of ours".(4) Grace, as Pope Francis neatly sums it up, tends to be tangible. The Eucharist is God's physical embrace, God's kiss of peace, if you will.

The teaching of the Church has always been clear that the sacraments are not magic. In the sacraments we are healed and transformed by the grace of the Holy Spirit, led ever more out of the entrapment in selfishness, which the Church calls original sin, as we become "partakers in the divine nature".(5) The sacraments *work*, that is they are efficacious, they are works of God. In the traditional formulation, the sacraments act *ex opere operato* (literally: "by the very fact of the action's being performed"). This means that the sacrament does not depend on the virtue of the celebrant, but on the power of God. Whenever the sacrament is celebrated in accordance with the intention of the Church, the Spirit acts in and through it. This is important teaching for those who (sometimes mockingly) ask the "what if" question about the unhinged priest who goes into a bakery and consecrates all the bread. Does anything sacramental happen? No. This is not in accordance with the intention of the Church.

An important point about the teaching on sacraments is that the fruits, or benefits, of the sacraments, also depend on the *disposition* of the one who receives them. The *Catechism* says that "celebrated worthily in faith, the sacraments confer the grace they signify".(6) Christ is at work in the sacraments, they are efficacious, but the extent to which they bear fruit in us depends on the disposition we bring. We don't just turn up and get an infusion of grace, like filling up a car with fuel. If we are unreconciled to our neighbour, or the Church, or involved in unjust practices, or are sitting there deeply ungrateful for the blessings of life and creation, then we are putting up our own barriers to the life that God is inviting us into. We need to be open to the power of the Holy Spirit. When dealing with all of this, sometimes the *Catechism* takes off in poetic flight, as if it recognises that metaphor is the best language to talk about God. On the effect on us of the sacraments, it says, "As fire transforms into itself everything it touches, so the Holy Spirit transforms into the divine life whatever is subjected to his power."(7)

The source and summit

There's no room in this book, sadly, to cover all the sacraments. For that, a good place to start is the *Catechism* or, for younger readers of any age, *YOUCAT*, the youth *catechism*. We'll concentrate here on the sacrament of the Eucharist and the role it plays in the *how* of being a Catholic Christian disciple of Jesus Christ today. There are a number of names for what we often call the Mass, or *Holy Mass*. This name in fact derives from the text of the Latin Mass, which ended with *"Ite, Missa Est"* meaning literally, "Go, it is the dismissal." We refer to the *Eucharist*, from the Greek word *eucharistein* meaning thanksgiving. The Eucharist is an action of thanksgiving to God. We also refer to the *Breaking of Bread*, since this is what Jesus did at the Last Supper, and was the action by which the two disciples at Emmaus recognised Jesus. It is also the expression the early Christians used to describe their Eucharistic assemblies (Acts 2:42). For a full list of the names we give to the Eucharist, see the *Catechism*, paragraphs 1328-1332.

The Eucharist has been described as a multi-faceted diamond, with many different aspects or dimensions to consider. The Constitution on Sacred Liturgy gives us a beautiful definition, which is worth quoting at length:

> At the Last Supper, on the night when He was betrayed, our Saviour instituted the Eucharistic Sacrifice of his Body and Blood. He did this in order to perpetuate the sacrifice of the Cross throughout the centuries until He should come again, and so to entrust to His beloved spouse, the Church, a memorial of His death and resurrection; a sacrament of love, a sign of unity, a bond of charity, a paschal banquet in which Christ is consumed, the mind is filled with grace, and a pledge of future glory is given to us.(8)

We sometimes recoil at the use of words like "sacrifice", but as we've noted already, it is central to the mystery of salvation. Since our experience of the global pandemic, we've been reminded that it is very much part of the human experience. We saw human beings literally offering up their own lives by working in situations of extreme risk in hospitals, staff in care homes living away from their families for months so as not to expose their residents to the virus, ordinary people turning up for work to keep the country going. In our "social liturgy" on a Thursday evening, we gave thanks on our doorsteps with antiphons of clapping and saucepan-banging. It was a communion of thanksgiving. In the Eucharist, the sacrifice (self-offering) of Jesus on the cross is perpetuated in time and space. There is only one sacrifice. What we witness and take part in is a sacramental re-presentation of that sacrifice. What comes over so strongly in the teaching of Vatican II is that this eucharistic sacrifice is not an event we witness, as if from afar. We should not be in attendance "as strangers or silent spectators".(9) This was the key shift brought about by the Council. We should "participate knowingly, devoutly, and actively".(10)

This does not just mean taking part in prayers and processions, important as that is; it means, above all, thanking God for the offering up of his Son, and learning "to offer ourselves too".(11) This is so important. This is an expression of our priesthood by virtue of our baptism. We are called to take part in the one priesthood of Christ. We are called to take part in his sacrifice by doing what he did, emptying ourselves in love and service, denying ourselves, devoting ourselves to the loving work of building a kingdom of peace and justice. The Mass, in those terms, is a profoundly counter-cultural sign, the antidote to a culture of individualism, status and power. In the Eucharist, it is not just the bread and wine which are transformed, or sanctified. If we are not being transformed by grace, through faith, then the Mass can certainly be no more than a ritual spectacle.

As we look now at the elements of the Mass, we will consider what they signify and how we might enter more deeply into being well disposed to take part. For Catholics like me who have been going to Mass for many years, there is a tendency to let it all become familiar, to stop engaging with the depths of the mystery. It's not always easy, especially if you're there with young children (and I've been there!), but over time, as and when you can, it's important to try and come back to a deeper formation in the faith.

The Introductory Rites

According to the *General Instruction on the Roman Missal* (*GIRM*), the Introductory Rites which precede the Liturgy of the Word have the character of a beginning, an introduction, and a preparation. The purpose of these rites, according to *GIRM*, "is to ensure that the faithful, who come together as one, establish communion and dispose themselves properly to listen to the Word of God and to celebrate the Eucharist worthily".(12) When the people gather for Mass on a Sunday – the Lord's Day – just who is it who is coming together? Well, not to put too fine a point on it, the Body of Christ. The Eucharist, as the *Catechism* reminds us, completes our Christian initiation. Having been "raised to the dignity of the royal priesthood by Baptism"(13) and configured more deeply to Christ in Confirmation, we participate with the whole community in the Lord's sacrifice of the Eucharist.

Introductory Rites

- Procession (with song)
- Sign of the Cross, Greeting
- (Brief Introduction)
- Penitential Rite
- Gloria (Sundays/feasts outside of Lent and Advent)
- Opening Prayer (Collect)

On our way into church, we dip our hand in holy water to remind us of our baptism, our ordination in the common priesthood of the faithful, the beginning of our journey of dying and rising with Christ. When we gather, we are reminded of our incorporation into the Body of Christ. In an era of identity politics, this has become an ever more important point. What joins us together as the Body of Christ is more central to who we are than any other *adjective* we place in front of us, much more significant than gender, race, age, nationality, or status. This is the point St Paul was making to the early Christians in Galatia. Now that they were "baptised into Christ" (Galatians 3:27) they were all children of God through faith. "There is no longer Jew or Greek, there is no longer slave or free, there is no longer male and female, for all of you are one in Christ Jesus" (Galatians 3:28). This would be a helpful starting point for engaging with identity politics, which so often arise from a genuine social injustice, but so often lead to division and people being confined in ever tighter constructs of identity.

Social justice, or right relations, was an issue right from the beginning of our celebrations of the Eucharist. In St Paul's stunning insight, there is no longer slave or free. Social statuses and the social injustices which flow from them are made irrelevant in the Body of Christ. All are forgiven, all are "let go" from versions of themselves which relied on strict identity markers "over against" another group or individual. The first Christians of Corinth struggled with this revolutionary concept. St Paul was the first to write about the Eucharist, perhaps only twenty years after the death and resurrection of Jesus. It is remarkable how quickly the Eucharist was established as a central practice of Christian life, even if some communities didn't quite get it. St Paul writes to the Corinthians to chide them. The early eucharistic gatherings took place in people's houses. In Corinth, it seems that the richer people were meeting first so that "one goes hungry and another becomes drunk" (1 Corinthians 11:21). To behave in this way was to show contempt for the Church and to "humiliate those who have nothing" (1 Corinthians 11:22). It was an unjust assembly; it was not really the Lord's supper.

In his wonderful book on the Eucharist, *Our One Great Act of Fidelity*, Ronald Rolheiser recalls the story of the famous historian Christopher Dawson whose aristocratic mother was grieved when he decided to convert to Catholicism. The reason? Not out of any great aversion to Catholic belief, but because now her son would have to "worship with the help".[14] His mother understood something fundamental about Catholicism, even though it is not always acted out in practice. The lord of the manor and the servant worship together in a profound equality. What we have generally struggled with is the relationship of equality in the Eucharist being carried over into the rest of our communal existence. Culture tends to trump religion. In the Acts of the Apostles, we have a vision of communal Christian life when, for a glorious while, culture and religion converged and "All who believed were together and had all things in common; they would sell their possessions and goods and distribute the proceeds to all, as any had need" (Acts 2:44-45). The routines of this early community give us a blueprint of the Christian life: "They devoted themselves to the apostles' teaching and fellowship, to the breaking of bread and the prayers" (Acts 2:42). A life of fellowship (*koinonia*) was a distinctive feature of this community, which gathered for the breaking of the bread, which shared all things in common, and looked after the vulnerable.

When the people gather for Mass, their sense of fellowship is enhanced by the singing of an entrance song, or hymn. This is what we missed so much in lockdown, and then when we could go to Mass again with no singing. We missed our expressions of fellowship. After the sign of the cross, the priest then greets the people with a simple formula, with one option being, "The Lord be with you." I've always been moved by the greeting which a bishop uses: "Peace be with you." This greeting, from a successor to the apostles, takes us right back to the upper room, when Jesus appeared to his frightened disciples and said those few short words, which said so much: you are reconciled with God, you are forgiven, you are loved. In the Penitential Act which follows, we are invited to acknowledge our sins. John Baldovin SJ makes the point that "the focus of the invitation is not so much our sinfulness as it is God's compassion and mercy".[(15)]

The third optional formula, which we don't often hear, puts the emphasis on the saving acts of Jesus: "You were sent to heal the contrite... You came to call sinners... You are seated at the right hand of the Father to intercede for us".[(16)] All of the three formulas end with an absolution, which is not the sacramental formula for penance. After the Gloria, one of the oldest Christian poetic compositions, which should be sung on all Sundays apart from during Lent and Advent, the priest invites the congregation to pray. At this point, as in other parts of the Mass, there should be silence (*GIRM*, 45), to remind ourselves that we are in God's presence, and to recollect our intentions. Then we have the Collect, in which the ancient Christian formula for prayer is used, that is prayer *to* the Father, *through* Christ, *in* the Holy Spirit. The stage is set for the Liturgy of the Word. The community has gathered as the Body of Christ, united in song, reflection, prayer and a recollection of God's loving mercy.

Liturgy of the Word

Vatican II reminded us of what is at the heart of The Road to Emmaus, that Christ is present in the broken bread of the sacrament and in his word. As it said so memorably in *Dei Verbum*: "The Church has always venerated the divine Scriptures just as she venerates the body of the Lord, since from the table of both the word of God and of the body of Christ she unceasingly receives and offers to the faithful the bread of life, especially in the sacred liturgy".[17] In addition, as the *General Instruction* reminds us, Christ is really present in the people gathered in his name and in the person of the minister. That is why, when we use incense, we venerate the people, the priest, the altar and the word of God.

Liturgy of the Word

- First Reading: Old Testament (or Acts of the Apostles in the Easter Season)
- Responsorial Psalm
- Second Reading: New Testament
- Gospel Acclamation
- Gospel
- Homily
- Profession of Faith
- Prayer of the Faithful

The Liturgy of the Word begins with a First Reading which is generally from the Old Testament. This is an innovation (or a restoration) of the Paul VI Mass. Before Vatican II, there were generally two readings, one from the Epistles of St Paul and one from the Gospel, and that was nearly always the Gospel of St Matthew. The Constitution on the Sacred Liturgy wanted to rekindle a love of sacred scripture in the faithful and urged more use of the Old Testament in the liturgy. Far from being ancient historical records, as we noted in the previous chapter, scripture speaks to us in the "today" of our lives in community. The *General Introduction to the Lectionary* underlines the importance of that concept when it says, "in the liturgy the Church faithfully adheres to the way Christ himself read and explained the Scriptures, beginning with the 'today' of his coming forward in the synagogue and urging all to search the Scriptures".[18]

After the other readings and acclamation, we have the Gospel reading, which the *GIRM* calls "the high point of the Liturgy of the Word".[19] The aesthetic or symbolic dimension of the liturgy of the word is important. At Mass, we use a Book of the Gospels, which contains the text of the four Gospels, as well as the lectionary, which contains all the readings. The Book of the Gospels should be suitably decorated and can be carried in the entrance procession by the deacon, although the lectionary may not. During the acclamation, the people stand as a sign of respect. Gesture and posture are central elements in the Mass. Today we might call it body language. We know how important that is, we know that we communicate through the language of our bodies. We see this dynamic at work in a football match. In moments of ecstasy, such as a goal, the crowd (at least the crowd that supports the team that scored) acts as one: on their feet, cheering, roaring, jumping, clapping. In a scene of discord, whether that's a difficult meeting, or a fraught family meal, the postures will all be different, out of sync. At Mass, the congregation maintains the same posture at the same time, as a sign of unity. We kneel together, sit together, stand together, except for those who are physically unable.

When it comes to the reading of the Gospel, things happen. We stand, candles and incense appear, we sing an acclamation. We turn to the ambo (lectern) and listen to the word of God. The power of this moment came home to me during a Mission Week which we held in school when I was headteacher. We were joined for the week by a group of Spiritan priests (formerly the Holy Ghost Fathers). At the concluding Mass, with the hall full of teenagers, Fr Patrick from Kenya danced to the ambo with the Book of the Gospels held aloft, light streaming in, while we all sang the acclamation in Swahili he had taught us earlier. The place, as they say, was rocking. I had goosebumps. I knew then that this was a moment in the Mass of beautiful importance. We were about to hear the word of God proclaimed to us and that meant something. That was a cause of joy. These "peak moments" don't happen very often for most of us at Mass, or in life for that matter, but when they do, they teach us something of lasting significance.

Baldovin reminds us that the fundamental dynamic of the Mass, in fact of all Christian liturgy, is proclamation and response: "First we receive God's self-communication (in this part of the Mass by means of the word of God) and this calls forth a response from us in terms of prayer and/or liturgical action".(20) We might also call this the ***why*** and ***how*** of Christian life. This dynamic is hard-wired in humanity's relationship with the divine: God calls in love, we respond in the broken voice of our humanity. We've noted this previously, but it's such a fundamental point it bears repeating. Everything we do for the good is a response to God's grace. Even our prayer is prompted by the Holy Spirit. This theology was hammered out in the fourth and early fifth centuries when Pelagius, an Irish monk, taught that there were ways in which we could save ourselves, or our own free will could initiate our response to grace. His main opponent in this mighty theological tussle was St Augustine. His view was that our salvation is always God's initiative, that we do nothing to earn it, we can only respond in gratitude. This was confirmed as orthodox (right teaching) by the Church at the Council of Carthage in AD 418.

Pope Francis came back to this theme in his exhortation, *Gaudete et Exsultate*. He warned about contemporary Pelagianism, within the Church especially, which regards the human will as capable of gaining God's grace, or worse still leads to a mindset that trusts in one's own powers and ideas. The Church, he reminds us, "has repeatedly taught that we are justified not by our own works or efforts, but by the grace of the Lord, who always takes the initiative".[21] We are justified, that is confirmed in right relations with God, reconciled with him, only by grace (Romans 3:24) through faith. We cannot merit this grace, even our cooperation in faith with it is "a prior gift of that same grace".[22] Pope Francis describes this as one of the great convictions of the Church and a key teaching for anyone who is engaged with the *how* of being a Catholic. Our *how* does not rely on our own efforts. Nor does it mean that we just sit back and wait for God to do the work. Once we have accepted this teaching, it is a source of joy as we recognise that our life and natural abilities are all God's gift. Everything is gift. "Only on the basis of God's gift, freely and humbly received, can we cooperate by our own efforts in our progressive transformation."[23]

This is the mindset, the disposition, which we must bring to the liturgy, which gives it the name Eucharist. We respond to the free gift of God with gratitude, an openness of heart to receive the free gift of God, so that his gift (grace) may grow and develop within us. If the life of God is growing in us, if we are cooperating with God's initiative, then it is expressed in love (works), which is the only way grace grows in us. As St Paul said, it is love which endures, it is love which gives us our deepest identity as a human being: "if I... do not have love, I am nothing" (1 Corinthians 13:2). In the Mass, following the Gospel proclamation, we see the pattern of our response unfold. In the Homily, the priest or deacon helps to interpret the scriptures so that they speak to the "today" of our circumstances. Baldovin comments that, "The homily connects what was proclaimed to the sacramental action which follows and the expression of that sacramental action in daily life."[(24)] The Eucharist is always oriented to our daily lives, to our commitment to extending the reign of God in our time and place.

Our response continues with the Creed, or Profession of Faith. This should not be some monotone restatement of what we believe, but is our assent to the word of God. Our response continues in The Prayer of the Faithful, another retrieval from the ancient form of the Eucharist (see: **The Eucharist in AD 150,** at the end of the chapter), which the *GIRM* informs us is the people "exercising an office of their baptismal priesthood".[(25)] We are praying with Christ for the salvation of the world. In particular, we are asked to pray "for the needs of the universal Church and the local community, for the salvation of the world and those oppressed by any burden, and for special categories of people".[(26)] Our response in prayer is an expression of our desire that the world may be more conformed to the Gospel. Our response in gratitude to the free gift of God's grace proclaimed in sacred scripture prepares us fittingly to enter into the Liturgy of the Eucharist, the first act of which continues our response to the proclamation as our gifts of bread and wine are brought to the altar.

Liturgy of the Eucharist

The *General Instruction* introduces the Liturgy of the Eucharist with a very helpful summary of the great pattern at the heart of this part of the Mass. It is worth quoting at length:

For Christ took the bread and the chalice, gave thanks, broke the bread and gave it to his disciples, saying: Take, eat and drink: this is my Body; this is the chalice of my Blood. Do this in memory of me.

Liturgy of the Eucharist

- The Preparation of the Gifts
- Prayer over the Offerings
- The Eucharistic Prayer
- The Communion Rite
- The Lord's Prayer
- The Rite of Peace
- The Fraction of the Bread
- Communion

Hence, the Church has arranged the entire celebration of the Liturgy of the Eucharist in parts corresponding to precisely these words and actions of Christ, namely:

> a. At the Preparation of the Gifts, bread and wine with water are brought to the altar, the same elements, that is to say, which Christ took into his hands.
>
> b. In the Eucharistic Prayer, thanks is given to God for the whole work of salvation, and the offerings become the Body and Blood of Christ.
>
> c. Through the fraction and through Communion, the faithful, though many, receive from the one bread the Lord's Body and from the one chalice the Lord's Blood in the same way that the Apostles received them from the hands of Christ himself.(27)

What we see here is what is sometimes called the "four-fold shape" of taking, blessing, breaking and giving. Baldovin comments that "the whole of the eucharistic action from the presentation of the gifts through Holy Communion is the acting out of the pattern given by Christ at the Last Supper".(28) This pattern, as some have pointed out, could be taken as the basic pattern of the Christian life (see: Rolheiser recommendation at the end of the chapter).

The gifts of bread and wine are brought to the altar in procession, as well as money collected from the people. There is a view that to bring money up with the gifts is somehow vulgar, but that misses the point, and also the tradition of the Eucharist going back to the earliest days. In the description of the Eucharist by Justin Martyr from around AD 150 (below), it is clear that an offering of money was part of the celebration and this was used to support the vulnerable. It might be more symbolically powerful if it was made known how much of the Sunday collection was going to support the poor and projects of justice. The faithful need to provide for the upkeep of the Church, indeed it is one of "The Precepts of the Church" (see: *Catechism* paragraphs 2041-2042), but in addition to that, one of the three responsibilities of the Church is the ministry of charity and there is no better place for that to be offered up than in the Eucharist.

When the altar has been prepared for the Liturgy of the Eucharist, the priest says a prayer of blessing for the gifts, modelled on the Jewish *berakah* blessing. This blessing acknowledges God as the true and only source of what we bring to the celebration. Sometimes these prayers are said silently, which I always think is a great pity, given their beauty. In the ancient world, the bread and wine that were brought forward were made by the community itself, which gave even more power and connection to the offering, but the symbolic value of the offering has if anything intensified over the years. The bread which is blessed is the "fruit of the earth and work of human hands".(29) We do not just bring the fruits of creation to be blessed and sanctified in the Mass, but more importantly, what we've done with them, how we have "tilled" and "kept" them.

We bring the "work of human hands" and that is subject to our flawed relations with each other and the earth. So much of the fruit of the earth, as we discussed in Chapter 1, is harvested with selfish intent, with no thought of replenishment, like the great forests of the Amazon. So much of the human effort to harvest the fruits of the earth is governed by unjust working conditions and exploitation. So much of the fruits of the earth is consumed in greed, with a great deal of waste, while many do not have enough to live on. So in the offering of bread we bring, if you like, the human condition, what Pope Francis calls "the cry of the earth and the cry of the poor".[30] We bring ourselves in all honesty, in gratitude for the riches of creation, in sorrow for its despoliation at our hands, in sorrow for the injustice visited on so many. We bring the human condition to the altar and pray that it will be sanctified and transformed in the offering of the Eucharist, that it will become for us the bread of life, our spiritual drink.

We then come to the Eucharistic Prayer, the high point and centre of the celebration, described by *GIRM* as a prayer of "thanksgiving and sanctification".[31] The main elements of the prayer unfold in a consistent pattern:

Thanksgiving. The word Eucharist means "thanksgiving". An "attitude of gratitude" governs the entire prayer. We are grateful for what God has done for us in Christ, for showing us that our fulfilment as human beings is in love, not rivalry and violence. The great prayers of the Church begin with invitation and response, another sign of unity, as when the priest invites us to "give thanks to the Lord our God" and we reply, "It is right and just".[32]

Acclamation. There are three acclamations in the Eucharistic Prayer, acts of faith filled with praise, which should ideally be sung: the "Holy Holy Holy" (also known as the "thrice Holy" or Sanctus), the memorial acclamation after the consecration and the Great Amen. The acclamation "Holy Holy Holy" is a wonderful reminder at this stage of the Mass that we are "surrounded by so great a cloud of witnesses" (Hebrews 12:1), the angels and saints in every time and place, as well as our sisters and brothers throughout the world, and those who have gone before us marked with the sign of faith.

Epiclesis. This Greek word literally means to "call on". It's a petition to the Lord to send the Holy Spirit down upon the gifts "so that they may become for us the Body and Blood of our Lord Jesus Christ".(33) Baldovin comments that this petition reminds us that "we do not control the sacramental presence of the Lord but can only beg for it – albeit with the complete assurance that God will be true to his promises".(34) The prayer reveals our total reliance on God's gift.

Institution narrative and Consecration. This is the most solemn moment of the Mass. The Lord's own words are used to identify the bread and wine with his Body and Blood. The Mass of Paul VI added "which will be given up for you" to the "word" over the bread. This adds greatly to the sense of self-offering and gift. The "word" over the chalice ends with, "which will be poured out for you and for many for the forgiveness of sins".(35) The scholarly consensus, according to Baldovin, is that "many" (from the Latin *multis*) is inclusive, not exclusive. The Aramaic term behind this has the sense of an exclamation, as in *how many!* The Institution narrative as we now have it does not match word for word any of the scriptural texts on which it is based. This is a prayer, formed in the tradition of the Church, based on the loving gift of Our Lord of himself at the Last Supper.

The accounts we have of the words at the Last Supper in the synoptic Gospels and St Paul are all slightly different, as you would expect from **Stage 3** writing (see: Chapter 5) which reflected the needs and traditions of their communities. What the Church highlights in her prayer – and the way the Church prays is prior to the way she believes – is that Christ's blood was poured out "for the forgiveness of sins". In the Eucharistic Prayer the sacrifice of our redemption is re-presented. Christ was made to "be sin" (2 Corinthians 5:21) so that we, all humanity, the human condition, may be reconciled to God: forgiven. Original sin is seen at its most stark at the crucifixion. The re-creation of the human condition from within which Jesus undertook in his ministry was too much for us. There was too much at stake, especially for those with power. We rejected the offer. We condemned and rejected love, we killed God. But our Victim has forgiven us, God has overturned our verdict and called us to a new way of being human. This was not done by some distant divine decree, but from within history. As Pope Benedict XVI said, "Christ took the lowest place in the world—the Cross—and by this radical humility he redeemed us."[(36)]

This is the sacrifice which is re-presented at the Mass. Baldovin reminds us of the "utter realism"[(37)] with which the Church has always understood the words of Jesus at the Last Supper. The Church teaches that at the Consecration the bread and wine *become* the Body and Blood of Jesus Christ. The Risen One is in our midst, sacramentally. The bread and wine have not changed chemically, but they have changed sacramentally, a gift of faith. In the classic philosophical language of St Thomas Aquinas, the "accidents" (appearances) are unchanged, but the "substance" (the essence of what they're about) has changed, so that it doesn't make sense to refer to them as bread and wine any more. The material elements are manifesting something else. The Risen One is in our midst.

Anamnesis. This Greek word means literally "remembrance". In the Last Supper accounts in St Paul and in the Gospel of St Luke,

Jesus commands his followers to "do this in remembrance of me" (1 Corinthians 11:23-26; Luke 22:15-20). It's a command to "participate again and again in a memorial of his death and resurrection by offering this prayer and sharing in the sacred sacrificial meal".[38] We're not just remembering the Last Supper, the way we might remember a significant family meal. We're "making memorial" – in the sense of making present again – the Paschal Mystery, the Passion, death and resurrection of the Lord, which the Eucharist re-presents in a sacramental manner.

Offering, or oblation. There is perhaps no other aspect of the Eucharist which has been as controversial as the idea of offering, or sacrifice. Who is offering what to whom? Why? Is an angry God being placated, is the devil's ransom being paid? The *GIRM* states that as well as the Church offering the "unblemished sacrificial Victim" to the Father, we must learn to offer our very selves, in other words to be like Jesus. This does not mean that we seek to die as he did, but it does mean that we follow the "way of the cross" which is the way of love, of self-emptying in love.

Intercessions. Prayers of intercession seem to have been present in the Eucharistic Prayer from very early on. It was as if, even though we had already said the Prayers of the Faithful, we wanted to express our needs in this holiest of moments, when the Risen Christ was among us. We pray for unity, we pray for the leaders of the Church, we pray with Mary the Mother of God, the apostles, the saints, the great company of witnesses, we pray for the dead. We pray, in the words of Eucharistic Prayer IV, that we may be free from original sin, from the "corruption of sin and death" and enter into a "heavenly inheritance"[39] which is the life of the new creation on earth.

Final doxology. All of the Eucharistic Prayers end with praise and glorification of God. This final prayer emphasises that

Christ is at the centre, that it is "through him, and with him and in him" that we seek our way to the Father, to fullness of life in the Holy Spirit. The prayer ends with another acclamation, the Great Amen, which is our participation, our affirmation, our "yes" to the Eucharistic Prayer.

Broken and given

The **Communion Rite** is part of the Liturgy of the Eucharist. In this rite, two of the "four-fold actions" of the Eucharist are found: breaking and giving. We are also reminded again of the "horizontal" aspect of the Body of Christ, represented by the people around us, as well as the eucharistic Body of Christ on the altar. We begin the Communion Rite with the **Lord's Prayer**, in which so much of what we have participated in is given voice. We celebrate our closeness to the Father, the origin of salvation, our oneness and equality in God. We ask for God's will, God's way, to be done on earth, as it is in heaven. We pray for "daily bread", the eucharistic bread we need to sustain us on the journey. We pray for forgiveness so that we may be worthy of receiving the Body of Christ and remind ourselves that the dynamic of forgiveness involves us forgiving those "who trespass against us". We cannot consider ourselves well disposed if we are "holding" others in our debt. We pray that we will be sustained through the temptations of daily life in a culture which will always try to seduce us into an existence of pleasure and status defined by social division.

Another great retrieval of the *Novus Ordo* from the ancient forms of the Mass was the **Sign of Peace**. The message is clear that we need to be reconciled – in right relation – with our neighbour in order to participate with integrity in Holy Communion. This wisdom is deeply embedded in the Christian tradition. Love of God and love of neighbour are interwoven. One is not possible without the other. In Matthew's Gospel Jesus advises the one who is on his way to worship but is not in right relation with others to "leave your gift there before the altar and go; first be reconciled to your brother or sister" (Matthew 5:24). **The breaking (or fraction) of the bread** which follows is richly symbolic. We've already seen in Chapter 5 that it's at the breaking of the bread that the two disciples at Emmaus recognise Jesus. This is his deepest reality: broken and shared for the life of the world. The breaking of the bread is accompanied by the saying or singing of the **Lamb of God**, in which again the prayer of the Church (*lex orandi*) leads to our belief (*lex credendi*) that in Jesus, the divine Victim, we have our liberation from "the sins of the world".[40]

At **Communion**, we have the third "action point" of the Mass, following on from the Entrance Procession and the Offertory Procession. Holy Communion is the high point of the Mass in terms of our participation. The people process to the altar to receive the Body and Blood of Christ. The *GIRM* says that "Holy Communion has a fuller form as a sign when it is received under both kinds."[41] This was lost during the pandemic and some may never go back to receiving Holy Communion under both kinds. Receiving only the host is certainly no "lesser" participation. For centuries the Church has maintained that to receive under one form we receive both the Body and Blood of the Lord ("concomitance"). I've always found the procession at Holy Communion a moving experience, to witness humanity in all its shapes and sizes humbly processing forward to receive the spiritual nourishment of the Risen Lord.

Communion should be received with reverence, with a bow, or for some a genuflection. We receive the Lord in our hands, or on our tongue. Some argue that to receive Holy

Communion on the tongue is more respectful, but for me the symbolism of extending both hands, one cupped over the other, palm upwards, strongly suggests that we are asking for, and receiving, a gift. The priest says, "The Body of Christ" and we respond in affirmation, "Amen." St Augustine, in one of his sermons to the newly baptised, said "Be what you see, and receive what you are."[(42)] This moment of intimate encounter does not need over-thinking. Intimacy is an experience, not an idea. The most appropriate prayer in a few moments of silence after Holy Communion is one of simple thanks to the Lord.

The Concluding Rites

The conclusion of the Mass is short and simple, almost anticlimactic after what has gone before, but in the Dismissal there is huge significance. We are invited to take into the world the peace we have encountered in the Mass, the love and reconciliation which has been proclaimed. The formulas for dismissal sum this up in various ways. The priest or deacon says, "Go and announce the Gospel of the Lord" or "Go in peace, glorifying the Lord by your life."[(43)] In other words, if we just go back to business as usual in the world, without any daily commitment to be transformed by the grace of God into a more loving disciple of Jesus, then it's really all been a waste of time. If we only go to Mass out of a sense of "obligation" or even (and I still hear this) out of fear of going to hell ("But Frank, is it still a mortal sin?"), then again, it's not the new life the Lord is inviting us into.

Our guide for this chapter, John Baldovin, says that we need to put flesh on the bones of our offering by the way we live our life. He refers to the work of Louis-Marie Chauvet who believes that "Christian identity rests on the tripod of Scripture, Sacrament and Ethics – all of which need to be balanced – and the tripod corresponds to the classic triad of the Greeks: Truth, Beauty and Goodness."[44] Like the body of Christ, we need to be "broken" and "shared" – broken not in the sense of self-harm, but in the sense of our own wills being broken, our own pride, our own sense of drive and achievement. We're "broken" when the levee of our pride is breached and the waters of grace flood our hearts. This is the effect of forgiveness in our lives. Then we have no option but to share this grace – which is God's own self – for the life of the world. The Church has always insisted that our "sending out" from Mass to proclaim the Gospel begins with good news to the poor. That good news is not just that those who are poor are loved, or even that Christians want to relieve their sufferings, but that the unjust structures which oppress them are not the will of God. As the *Catechism* says, the Church's preferential option for the poor means that Christians are committed to the "relief, defence and liberation"[45] of those who are oppressed by various forms of poverty.

St John Chrysostom, in the third century, left his congregation in no doubt about the right relation between the body of the Lord in the Eucharist and the poor: "Do you wish to honour the body of the Christ? Do not ignore him when he is naked. Do not pay him homage in the eucharist clad in silk only then to neglect him outside where he suffers cold and nakedness".[46] Jesus has forever associated himself with the hungry, the thirsty, the stranger, the sick, the prisoner, those who are oppressed by injustice. In as much as we walk with them and work for their liberation, we walk with Jesus (Matthew 25:31-46). The *Catechism* puts it this way: "The Eucharist commits us to the poor. To receive in truth the Body and Blood of Christ given up for us, we must recognize Christ in the poorest, his brethren".[47]

A commitment to social justice is not a special reserve for "activists" in the Church. It is the heart of the Gospel. As we read in Chapter 3, original sin and personal sin have social consequences in unjust and distorted relationships. Redemption, therefore, has a social dimension. It is not a private arrangement; it is universal and integral. St Paul described the Christian community as one in which unjust social relations ("slave and free") were ended in the equality of the children of God. Dignity was restored. The mission of the Church is to take this good news to the world, to be "catalysts for the redemption and transformation of social relationships".[48] The world as God envisages it, as Jesus showed us in his life and ministry, is a world of peace and justice, not a world of oppressive relations where some thrive at the cost of many. The Lord we encounter in the Eucharist is the one who comes through the locked doors of the human condition, to find fearful humans who struggle with the idea that they can be loved. He breathes peace on us, the power of his Spirit to go out and be ambassadors for a new way of being and belonging.

A note on the Eucharistic Prayers

We're probably familiar with four Eucharistic Prayers. I remember when I was younger that sense of relief when the priest said, "Eucharistic Prayer No. 2…" because it was the shortest. There are in fact ten Eucharistic Prayers in total. As well as the four we are familiar with, there are prayers for use with children (which really should be used in school), two Eucharistic Prayers for reconciliation and what is called "Eucharistic Prayers for Use in Masses for Various Needs" which have four variations. One is called "Jesus, who went about doing good". It's a pity we don't hear them more often. They are beautiful prayers in themselves, which you'll find in most Sunday Missals. Here's an extract from the one I just mentioned:

"Open our eyes
to the needs of our brothers and sisters;
inspire in us words and actions
to comfort those who labour and are burdened.
Make us serve them truly,
after the example of Christ and at his command.
And may your Church stand as a living witness
to truth and freedom,
to peace and justice,
that all people may be raised up to a new hope."[49]

The Eucharist in AD 150

"On the day called Sunday, all who live in the cities or in the country gather together to one place, and then memoirs of the apostles or the writings of the prophets are read, as long as time permits; then, when the reader has ceased, the president verbally instructs and exhorts to the imitation of these good things.

Then we all rise together and pray and... when our prayer is ended, bread and wine and water are brought, and the president in like manner offers prayers and thanksgiving, according to his ability, and the people assent, saying Amen; and there is a distribution to each, and a participation of that over which thanks have been given, and to those who are absent a portion is sent by the deacons.

And they who are well to do, and willing, give what each thinks fit; and what is collected is deposited with the president, who succours the orphans and widows, and those who, through sickness or any cause are in want, and those who are in bonds, and the strangers sojourning among us, and in a word takes care of all who are in need."

Justin Martyr, *The First Apology*[50]

"We cannot love God unless we love each other, and to love we must know each other. We know him in the breaking of bread, and we know each other in the breaking of bread, and we are not alone any more. Heaven is a banquet and life is a banquet, too, even with a crust, where there is companionship."

Dorothy Day[51]

HOW

Practical suggestions and resources for growing in faith through the liturgy, especially participation in the Eucharist

For a detailed study of the elements of the Mass, I'd recommend you go to the *General Instruction on the Roman Missal*. This document from the Vatican, adapted to local contexts by Bishops' Conferences, was revised most recently in 2003. A PDF version can be found on the website of the Liturgy Office of the Bishops' Conference of England and Wales at: https://www.liturgyoffice.org.uk/Resources/GIRM/Documents/GIRM.pdf (accessed August 2021).

The other key document of introduction to be aware of is the General Introduction to the Lectionary, which deals specifically with the Liturgy of the Word, and can be found at: http://www.liturgyoffice.org.uk/Resources/Rites/Lectionary.pdf (accessed August 2021). These documents should be central to any formation programme.

There are many good books on the Eucharist. I'd recommend three which I have found particularly useful:

Why Go To Church? by Timothy Radcliffe. This book is written in a very engaging and accessible style, and roots the experience of the Eucharist in the events of our times.

Our One Great Act of Fidelity by Ronald Rolheiser. This book is shorter, and also very accessible. It covers the different dimensions of the Eucharist, such as sacrifice, memorial, washing of the feet, invitation to justice, priestly prayer. There is also an extended meditation on the "four-fold shape" of the Eucharist – *taking, blessing, breaking and giving*.

Bread of Life, Cup of Salvation by John F. Baldovin. This book, which I have quoted throughout this chapter, is a more systematic survey of the history, theology and elements of the Eucharist. There is also an extended theological reflection.

Chapter SIX References

1. Second Vatican Council, *Sacrosanctum Consilium* (Constitution on the Sacred Liturgy), 10
2. Pope Francis, *Laudato Si'* (On Care for our Common Home), 234
3. Pope Francis, *Laudato Si'*, 236
4. Pope Francis, *Laudato Si'*, 236
5. *CCC*, 1129
6. *CCC*, 1127
7. *CCC*, 1127
8. *Sacrosanctum Consilium*, 47
9. *Sacrosanctum Consilium*, 48
10. *Sacrosanctum Consilium*, 48
11. *Sacrosanctum Consilium*, 48
12. *GIRM*, 46
13. *CCC*, 1322
14. Ronald Rolheiser, *Our One Great Act of Fidelity* (New York: Doubleday, 2011), 73
15. John F. Baldovin SJ, *Bread of Life, Cup of Salvation: Understanding the Mass* (Maryland: Rowman and Littlefield Publishers Inc., 2003), 73
16. *Your Sunday Missal* (Chawton: Redemptorist Publications, 2011), 453
17. Second Vatican Council, *Dei Verbum* (Dogmatic Constitution on Divine Revelation), 21
18. *General Introduction to the Lectionary*, 3
19. *GIRM*, 60
20. Baldovin, *Bread of Life*, 93
21. *Gaudete et Exsultate*, 52
22. *Gaudete et Exsultate*, 53
23. *Gaudete et Exsultate*, 56
24. Baldovin, *Bread of Life*, 83
25. *GIRM*, 69

26. *GIRM*, 30
27. *GIRM*, 72
28. Baldovin, *Bread of Life*, 98
29. *Your Sunday Missal*, 460
30. *Laudato Si'*, 49
31. *GIRM*, 72
32. *Your Sunday Missal*, 471
33. *Your Sunday Missal*, 472
34. Baldovin, *Bread of Life*, 118
35. *Your Sunday Missal*, 472
36. *Deus Caritas Est*, 35
37. Baldovin, *Bread of Life*, 118
38. Baldovin, *Bread of Life*, 120
39. *Your Sunday Missal*, 483
40. *Your Sunday Missal*, 486
41. *GIRM*, 281
42. Quoted in Rolheiser, *Our One Great Act of Fidelity*, 130
43. *Your Sunday Missal*, 489
44. Baldovin, *Bread of Life*, 160
45. CCC, 2448
46. Baldovin, *Bread of Life*, 175
47. CCC, 1397
48. *Compendium of the Social Doctrine of the Church*, 52
49. *Your Sunday Missal*, 554
50. A. Roberts and J. Donaldson, *The Ante-Nicene Fathers* (Buffalo: The Christian Literature Publishing Company, 1885), 186
51. Dorothy Day, *The Long Loneliness* (New York: HarperCollins, 1952), 285

Chapter 7

Prayer,

"God's desire for us"

There are two main types of prayer, what the *Catechism* calls "the prayer of the Church and personal prayer",[1] otherwise known as liturgical prayer and devotional prayer. The difference between the two is summed up very neatly by Ronald Rolheiser: "Devotional prayer… is private in nature and is meant to help sustain us personally on the spiritual journey. Liturgical prayer, by contrast, is public in nature, is the Church's prayer (not our own), is universal in scope, and is intended for the needs of the world".[2] So, "devotional" prayer (sometimes also called "affective" prayer) is personal, about our needs, whereas "liturgical" prayer (sometimes also called "priestly" prayer) is not about us, although we are involved and participate. It's about the world, and for the world. Rolheiser provides some examples to help us distinguish between the two. You could have five hundred people meditating together in a hall, or saying the rosary at a shrine. That is still personal, or devotional prayer. On the other hand, you could have a priest celebrating Mass alone at a kitchen table, or on a mountain, or someone praying the Divine Office in an armchair at home, and that is still public, liturgical prayer, the prayer of the Church. What we'll be looking at in this chapter is devotional, or affective prayer, and how it might sustain us on the journey of discipleship.

We enter into personal prayer the way we enter into the liturgy, "by the narrow gate of faith".[3] We've already noted that faith is the gateway virtue. In faith, we approach Our Lord with a heart which is open, not fearful or suspicious. A heart which knows that we are not in charge: we are the creature, not the Creator; the guest, not the host. A heart which is ready to be changed, stretched into a bigger and more generous existence, "a heart open to the whole world".[4] A heart which is the locus of prayer. The *Catechism* takes a resolutely scriptural approach to prayer and acknowledges that while the soul or spirit is mentioned, "According to Scripture, it is the *heart* that prays."[5] The heart, or the formation of the heart, has been our central theme, so it's worth quoting at length the *Catechism's* definition:

> The heart is the dwelling-place where I am, where I live… the heart is the place 'to which I withdraw'. The heart is our hidden centre, beyond the grasp of our reason and of others; only the Spirit of God can fathom the human heart and know it fully. The heart is the place of decision, deeper than our psychic drives. It is the place of truth, where we choose life or death. It is the place of encounter, because as image of God we live in relation: it is the place of covenant.[6]

St Paul tells his community in Corinth around AD 50 that their body is "a temple of the Holy Spirit within you" (1 Corinthians 6:19). In that case, the heart is the "holy of holies" of our body, the place of encounter with the living God, just as the Holy of Holies in the First Temple was the place of encounter once a year between the High Priest and God. Just as the First Temple Holy of Holies housed the ark of the covenant, so our heart is the place of covenant, the unbreakable bond between us and our loving Creator. No matter what we do, this covenant holds, his love lasts for ever. We are made "in the image of God" (Genesis 1:27), made for relationship with each other and above all with the Trinity, the communion of love. This knowledge is deeper than reason, the kind of *knowing* that is more like the intimacy between lovers than the knowledge of the mind. It is more felt than thought.

Christian prayer is a covenant relationship, and like any relationship it needs to be sustained by both partners. There is no danger of God ever tiring of his commitment to this relationship. He is steadfast and true. We are the ones who are unreliable, who will drift away, forget the mighty deeds of the Lord. We are the ones who need to work on this, so let us look at the features of this relationship and how it might be sustained. Our chief guide in this chapter is the *Catechism of the Catholic Church* and the saints. You will have your own image of the *Catechism*. For me, growing up as a cradle Catholic, it was a chore, a text to be learned by rote. It was never something I associated with poetry or inspiration. For most of my adult life in the faith I didn't read much of the *Catechism*, prejudiced by that early view that it was juridical and dull. Until, that is, I began to look more deeply into prayer and I realised that one quarter of the *Catechism* (Part Four) is devoted to Christian Prayer. What I found there was a revelation. Far from dry, moralistic formulations, I found a text of rich teaching, which at times sounded more like poetry than anything else, as we've just seen in the extract on the heart.

What is prayer?

If we enter into prayer through the narrow gate of faith, then like all virtues, that implies that habit is involved. Faith is a habit, a disposition which God is working to instil in us. Therefore, "the life of prayer is the habit of being in the presence of the thrice-holy God and in communion with him".[7] The Catholic Church, unlike some other faiths, does not prescribe a daily prayer pattern for the laity. If you were a monk, your prayer pattern would be governed by the "hours" of the Divine Office. Although Lauds (morning prayer) and Vespers (evening prayer) are increasingly popular among lay Catholics, they are not an expectation, or a rule of being a Catholic. There is in the Christian tradition a treasure house of resources for prayer, but "The Lord leads all persons by paths and in ways pleasing to him, and each believer responds according to his heart's resolve and the personal expressions of his prayer."[8]

This means that, unlike liturgy, which we don't change if it doesn't suit us, we can change our devotional practices. We can search in the storehouse of Christian tradition until we find a practice, or practices, that work for us, that resonate with our personality, our lifestyle, our state in life. We believe that in this search, as in every other aspect of the spiritual life, we are guided by the Spirit. We'll look in this chapter at some expressions, forms and practices of prayer which might be used, but in the end the Church leaves it between the person and their Lord to work out what suits them best. What is less negotiable is that it should be a habit. Not something you turn to when you feel like it, or when you're in trouble, but routinely, daily. In the *Didache*, one of the earliest manuals of the Church, dating from perhaps as early as AD 100, the advice to Christians was to pray the Our Father three times a day – morning, noon and night. In the early Church, daily prayer would have been the norm, as it was for observant Jews.

In the *Catechism*, in answer to the question, "What is prayer?", after the perhaps overly familiar response from the *Penny Catechism* of "the raising of one's mind and heart to God or the requesting of good things from God",[9] we find this: "The wonder of prayer is revealed beside the well where we come seeking water: there, Christ comes to meet every human being. It is he who first seeks us and asks us for a drink. Jesus thirsts;

his asking arises from the depths of God's desire for us".[10] This wonderful description of prayer takes us back to that vivid scene in John's Gospel when Jesus is slumped by a well at midday. He is tired. The disciples have gone off into the village to buy food. A woman comes to the well with her empty jar – a woman with a complicated past, a woman on her own in the hottest part of the day, a woman that the other women might avoid. It is to this woman that Jesus says, "Give me a drink" (John 4:7). He shouldn't have been speaking to her. He has crossed all sorts of cultural and religious barriers to start this conversation, as a man, as a Jew (she is a Samaritan), and yet this is the encounter that the *Catechism* holds up to us as a description of prayer.

God is thirsting for us, no matter how unworthy or unready we regard ourselves as being. All we have to do is come to the well with our empty jars. "Humility is the foundation of prayer."[11] God calls first. It is always that way round. Gift and response. We are not in charge here, in the way we often feel we are in our lives, reliant on our own skills and determination to succeed. That is of no use whatsoever in the life of prayer. We do not climb the ladder to heaven by our own efforts. As we observed in Chapter 1, the Bible is more about God's search for us than our search for God. We saw that in God's tender question to the fallen Adam and Eve, "Where are you?" (Genesis 3:9). At that moment, they don't know where they are, they have lost confidence in God and are hiding from him, naked and ashamed. Before they leave the garden, God made garments for them, he "clothed them" (Genesis 3:21) for their life's journey "East of Eden". We've been wrapped in that divine care ever since, even though we often forget.

And there he prayed

God did not abandon human beings to fruitless wandering in a valley of tears after the Garden of Eden, that dream of communion with God. He sent us prophets and witnesses of hope, comfort and encouragement – and of course of chastisement – but more than that, he sent his only Son, the Word made flesh to be among us and tell us how to be friends with God. He showed us what God was like, a God of steadfast love and forgiveness. When we see Jesus in the Gospels, we not only see God, we see ourselves as we should be in the likeness of God. And Jesus prays. At the beginning of Mark's Gospel, after a day of healing many who were brought to him with sickness and demons, we hear that "in the morning, while it was still very dark, he got up and went out to a deserted place, and there he prayed" (Mark 1:35). Jesus prays often, it is a habit for him. He does not pray as a display, he does not lead daily community prayer; the disciples have to prompt him to teach them how to pray, like John taught his disciples. He prays on his own, in the silence before dawn, to his Father who calls him "Beloved" and whom he calls "Abba" – an Aramaic word for "father" connoting great trust, affection and closeness. The prayer of Jesus is the encounter with his Father, whose will is his life's mission: the relationship that gives meaning to his earthly life.

In Matthew's Gospel, Jesus does give us some instructions about prayer. He tells us to avoid letting everybody know when we're being pious – like the hypocrites, those who live in the eyes of others. He says to us – "go into your room and shut the door and pray to your Father who is in secret" (Matthew 6:6). He knows what we're like, that we're needy creatures, always looking for the affirmation of others to keep us alive. He knows that we're manipulative, that we're skilled at getting our own way at the expense of the truth. All that needs to be left at the door when we enter our "inner room", the place where no one sees us. We do not need to go to church to be in the presence of God. A quiet corner anywhere will do fine. And when we get there, we can drop the mask, forget the speeches. Jesus says when you pray, "do not heap up empty phrases as the Gentiles do; for they think that they will be heard because of their many words. Do not be like them, for your Father knows what you need before you ask him" (Matthew 6:7-8). Our Father is attentive and knows what we need for fullness of life. Our journey in prayer is to become like Jesus, transparent to the will of the Father, to be "drawn" (John 6:44) to him, not pulled further into the futility of our own desires.

So, from scripture and from tradition we have some good advice about what prayer is and how to go about praying. It is God's first step towards us. St Paul says it is the Spirit of God praying in us, helping us in our weakness. We really don't know what we're doing in the presence of the Holy One, "we do not know how to pray as we ought" (Romans 8:26). The very desire to pray is God's Spirit at work in us, drawing us to himself. Prayer is friendship with God, wasting time with God, if you like, because we have nowhere more important to be. Prayer is not weaving clever phrases in the hope of bending God's will to what we think we need. God knows what we need, and it is not always what we think we need. Prayer is poverty, simplicity, honesty. It is making room for God, growing in participation in God's own life, which is why it leads to loving action in the world. Jesus did not spend his entire life in the wilderness as a contemplative. In the wilderness, led by the Spirit, his mission was made clear to him. Then it was time to begin his public ministry. His prayer fuelled his mission, inspired his decisions, expressed his hopes and fears, his sense of who he was and what he was called to do, "to seek out and to save the lost" (Luke 19:10).

People who pray are sometimes accused of wasting time, especially when there is a situation of urgent need. This has never been the Christian view. Pope Benedict XVI says, "Piety does not undermine the struggle against the poverty of our neighbours."[12] He cites the examples of St Teresa of Calcutta, who worked in circumstances of extreme poverty, as "a clear illustration of the fact that time devoted to God in prayer not only does not detract from effective and loving service to our neighbour but is in fact the inexhaustible source of that service".[13] Benedict was responding to what he saw as the "activism and the growing secularism of many Christians engaged in charitable work".[14] It may be well-intentioned, but it is not the work of the Church if it is not rooted in prayer and inspired by the values of the Gospel. The "activist" mindset might say, "what's the point of praying, are you trying to change God's mind? It doesn't look as if that approach has been very successful over the years." Benedict agrees with this to some extent. The Christian who prays, "does not claim to be able to change God's plans or correct what he has foreseen".[15] The point of prayer is an encounter with God, asking for the presence and consolation of God in the midst of difficult circumstances. The point of prayer is to make more and more space for God and less and less for our own ideas. We are praying to see the world as God does, with eyes of compassion. That is the starting point for all charity.

Expressions and forms of prayer

In the Christian tradition there are three major *expressions of prayer*: vocal, meditative and contemplative. What they all have in common is remembering God, not becoming consumed by the business of Monday morning, or the pleasures of Friday night, with Sunday the only time when God gets a look in. "Prayer is a remembrance of God."[16] That is why it is important that prayer is a habit, on a Monday morning and a Friday night, as much as on a Sunday. The three great expressions of prayer could be a description of the journey of prayer itself, tending more and more towards silence. But words are a good place to start, even if we don't need too many. After all, Jesus taught his disciples a vocal prayer, the Our Father. It's not a long prayer, which is significant. It doesn't have to be. But praying "out loud" is honoured by Jesus himself as such an important part of our relationship with God. What we need to be wary of is vocal prayer which is disconnected from the heart. Rote prayer, the kind of prayer we rattle through. As Jesus said in Mark's Gospel, quoting Isaiah, "This people honours me with their lips, but their hearts are far from me" (Mark 7:6). It is important that "the heart should be present to him to whom we are speaking in prayer".[17] Vocal prayer is at the heart of the liturgy, of course, but heartfelt vocal prayer is also the first step in devotional prayer. We can pray out loud in groups, using prayers from the devotional treasure box of the Church, or more modern prayers, or improvised prayers for an occasion. We can also pray out loud in our "inner room", speaking to God as a friend.

As well as the expressions of prayer (and we'll come back to meditative and contemplative prayer), there are *five forms of prayer* associated mostly with vocal prayer which are normative in the Christian tradition, drawn from scripture: Blessing and Adoration; Petition; Intercession; Thanksgiving; Praise. There is no room in this brief survey to cover them all, and some aspects were covered in previous chapters. At the end of this chapter, I have signposted some resources for further study and of course the *Catechism* offers teaching on them all. I'll just concentrate for now on petition, or supplication. This is the most human prayer in which we "ask, beseech, plead, invoke, entreat, cry out, even 'struggle in prayer'".[18] A moving example of the prayer of supplication in the Gospels is when the Canaanite woman whose daughter is tormented by a demon kneels before Jesus and simply says, "Lord, help me" (Matthew 15:25). Initially, Jesus ignored her, since she was not one of the lost sheep of the House of Israel he had come to save. But he is moved by her great faith. Jesus is not indifferent to the pleas of humanity.

Prayers of petition tend to be short. The most well-known in the Christian tradition, especially in the Orthodox Church, is the *Jesus Prayer,* based on the humble prayer of the Tax Collector in Luke's Gospel who, unlike the Pharisee, brings only his poverty to his prayer (Luke 18:13). The most common form of the prayer is, "Lord Jesus Christ, Son of God, have mercy on me a sinner." It is the simplest way of praying often, at any point in the day. It contains so much of what should be at the heart of prayer: a humble turning to God, an acknowledgement of the need of God's mercy. It is not the heaping up of empty phrases, it acts as a "block" on the other random and often unhelpful thoughts which tend to fill our minds. Prayers of petition for others are intercessions and in the Christian tradition we also pray to the saints, to Mary the Mother of God, to intercede for the needs of those we love, and those we struggle to love. We know that our prayers are heard but we do not always know how they are answered. God is not an ATM who produces what we want when we insert our card. The purpose of prayers of intercession is to enlarge our hearts to think of the needs of others. In prayer we grow in communion with God and the gifts we receive in prayer help us to be a better friend, neighbour, spouse and so on. It's not a magic fix for the needs of others.

Petition is the most usual form of prayer because it's the most spontaneous. It is our turning to God, "the expression of a heart that trusts in God and realizes that of itself it can do nothing".[19]

Not to pray is to be enclosed in ourselves, which is not natural. The prayer of petition puts us in right relation with God. It is real and raw. "Give us this day our daily bread" (Matthew 6:11). It is not about putting on what we used to call our best "telephone manner". Denis McBride comments that this movement out of silence is deeply rooted in biblical tradition, "That people should express their suffering in lamentation, not repress it in brooding silence".[20] This "silence breaking" is the first step towards justice, by expressing the wrong. How we pray is how we believe, saying it out loud is an important part of our faith. Our prayer should come out of where we are, whether that's gratitude or grievance. In the Psalms in particular we see the full range of human emotion on display, including the distress of innocent suffering:

> Even now they lie in wait for my life;
> the mighty stir up strife against me.
> For no transgression or sin of mine, O Lord,
> for no fault of mine, they run and make ready.
>
> (Psalm 59:3-4)

There have been so many times in history when human beings have walked in the valley of darkness, when they have cried out, "Why Lord?" When the suffering of the innocent made us doubt our faith in a loving God.

The suffering of the Jewish people in the Holocaust, with the systematic execution of six million men, women and children in the gas chambers, is a crime that cries out to heaven. We cannot ever be glib in our theology of suffering. There are no clear answers. But we can look to the wisdom of those who suffered. Elie Wiesel's account of his imprisonment in Auschwitz is among the most powerful testimonies of the Holocaust. In one harrowing scene in his memoir, *Night,* he recalls the day when two men and a boy were chosen for execution by hanging in reprisal for the discovery of weapons among the prisoners. All the prisoners were made to march past and look at the grim spectacle:

> The two men were no longer alive. Their tongues were hanging out, swollen and bluish. But the third rope was still moving: the child, too light, was still breathing...
>
> And so he remained for more than half an hour, lingering between life and death, writhing before our eyes. And we were forced to look at him at close range. He was still alive when I passed him. His tongue was still red, his eyes not yet extinguished.
>
> Behind me, I heard some man asking:
>
> "For God's sake, where is God?"

In the horror of the very worst that human beings can do to one another, our one remaining prayer sometimes is, "Where are you, God?" And yet, even in these moments of the deepest darkness and despair, sometimes faith is found. Wiesel continues:

> And from within me, I heard a voice answer:
>
> "Where is He? This is where – hanging here from these gallows..."(21)

Lawrence Kushner, a rabbi and widely read author on Jewish spirituality, when dealing with the question of God and the Holocaust says, "The question is not Where was God? But Why do human beings do such things? Blaming God not only absolves us but increases the likelihood that we will allow such horrors to happen again."(22)

He goes on to say that God did not die in the Holocaust but rather what died was the "Deuteronomic idea"(23) of a God who rewards and punishes people by suspending the laws of nature (as in the Exodus account of the drowning of the Egyptians). Divine interventions of this kind were meant to be seen as metaphors, not the way God works in history. The sun rises on the just and the unjust alike. To ask why God didn't do anything to stop the horror assumes that sometimes in the past he did, but that is not the image of God we're left with after the Holocaust.

The question which haunts the human imagination is "Why did God not create a world so perfect that no evil could exist in it?" Of course, were such a state to exist then we'd be none the wiser, we would only know what we knew. We wouldn't know good from its opposite, there would only be a bland blissful norm. The *Catechism* puts it this way, "with infinite wisdom and goodness God freely willed to create a world 'in a state of journeying' towards its ultimate perfection".(24) The Christian tradition distinguishes between physical evil and moral evil. Physical evil, which arises from a creation which is not perfect, includes all that harms human beings, such as natural disasters and misfortune. Kushner makes the point that in these circumstances human choices can diminish the impact considerably: "How much misery might be prevented, for instance, if humanity chose to allocate its resources toward healing rather than war?"(25) In the Covid pandemic (assuming that the evidence tells us it was a "natural" occurrence), think of how much suffering would have been prevented had societies been ordered in a more just and compassionate way, with significant investment in healthcare and the prevention of disease; if governance always considered the common good.

The other type of evil is moral evil. The story of Adam and Eve in the garden is the narrative account of how moral evil came into the world, when human beings turned from God and grasped at a wisdom and a power which breached his prohibitions. God is not the cause of moral evil, we are. God permits moral evil, because to do otherwise would mean we had no freedom and were controlled by divine agency. God permits even our moral evil because he respects our freedom and he knows that good will come of it, which we have seen consistently in history. The *Catechism* describes the crucifixion as "the greatest moral evil ever committed", caused by "the sins of all men".[26] In other words, as we have said, the crucifixion is the most dramatic revelation of – and simultaneous forgiveness of – original sin.

> By his Passion, Christ delivered us from Satan and from sin. He merited for us the new life in the Holy Spirit. His grace restores what sin has damaged in us.[27]

Jesus did not spend much time explaining the great questions of evil. He made it clear that physical evil was not any kind of judgement of God (Luke 13:4; John 9:3). He took on moral evil (became sin) and filled it with his presence. Perhaps the most raw and heart-rending example of Jesus speaking out of the human condition towards heaven is the "loud cry" (Mark 15:37) of pain and desolation that breaks from him on the cross. The *Catechism* tells us that "all the troubles, for all time, of humanity enslaved by sin and death, all the petitions and intercessions of salvation history are summed up in this cry of the incarnate Word".[28] It is the primal prayer of humankind, the cry of all the pain and heartbreak we've ever suffered. The cry of injustice, the cry of the victim.

And it has an answer. The answer does not come on that dark Friday afternoon outside the walls of Jerusalem on a grim execution site. On the morning of the new creation, Easter Sunday, "beyond all hope", the Father answers this cry "by raising his Son".[29] Despair does not have the last word. We are invited into a new life, invited to take part in the building up of a kingdom of forgiveness, peace and justice where the effects of physical and moral evil can be diminished.

Meditation

We are called to a better way of being human, we are called to be holy. In the past, it may have seemed that holiness was the preserve of the religious professionals, the saints and the mystics, and the rest of us just got on with the business of living in the real world. *Lumen Gentium* set the record straight, once and for all: "Everyone in the church is called to holiness".[30] This holiness is within our reach. It is not easy, but it is our calling as human beings. "Holiness is nothing other than charity lived to the full."[31] It is a calling to be loving in the midst of an ordinary life. As Pope Francis says, "Do you work for a living? Be holy by labouring with integrity and skill in the service of your brothers and sisters."[32] Holiness is nourished by prayer as well as loving action in the world. Pope Francis continues, "I do not believe in holiness without prayer, even though that prayer need not be lengthy or involve intense emotions."[33]

It's not easy to find the necessary balance between prayer and activity. As it says in the parable of the sower, sometimes the word of God is "choked by the cares and riches and pleasures of life" (Luke 8:14). We need to make time, find time, to step back from the cares of the world, the "rat race" as it used to be called. I once heard somebody say that if you are too busy to pray then that is in fact idolatry, since you're saying that everything else is more important than God. That might seem a bit harsh, especially if you have young children and have to work long hours to look after them. But as Pope Francis said, prayer doesn't have to be lengthy. The main point we keep coming back to is that it has to be routine. When it comes to meditation, there are methods which are rooted in Christian tradition, but do not require long hours on our knees. It doesn't take very long to "face our true selves and let the Lord enter".[34]

Meditation is a quest in which "the mind seeks to understand the why and how of the Christian life, in order to adhere and respond to what the Lord is asking".[35] Meditation, like holiness, is not just for the professionals. There are many ways to meditate, to engage thought, imagination, emotion and desire. The purpose of meditation is "to deepen our convictions of faith, prompt the conversion of our heart and strengthen our will to follow Christ".[36] Christian prayer tries to meditate above all on the mysteries of the life of Christ in ***Lectio Divina***, which we looked at in Chapter 5, and in the **rosary**, a much-cherished form of Catholic devotional prayer. The *Catechism* also directs our attention to a type of meditation which it calls "the book of life".[37] This meditation discerns "the movements that stir the heart"[38] and helps us to answer the question, "Lord, what do you want me to do?"[39] I think the best example of this kind of meditation is found in the Jesuit tradition, in the prayer called the **Examen**.

St Ignatius of Loyola, who founded the Jesuit Order (The Society of Jesus), was born in the Spanish Basque country into a noble family in 1491. By his own account, he was something of a dissolute youth, a vain, hot-headed gambler and womaniser. His behaviour was so rowdy during Mardi Gras in 1515 (what we call Shrove Tuesday, an excuse for a final binge before Lent) that he was pursued by the local magistrate and just about got away with it by fleeing to the Bishop of Pamplona for protection. Ignatius dreamed of chivalrous accomplishment and claiming the hand of a lady in court. In 1521, he got his chance to prove himself in battle. French troops marched on Pamplona and Ignatius was one of a small Spanish garrison left to guard the city. Most of the garrison sensibly opted to surrender, but Ignatius was having none of that. With a rousing speech, he persuaded the commander to make a last stand. It didn't end well for Ignatius when a French cannonball smashed into his legs and he was carried home on a stretcher in a great deal of pain. Over the next few months, he underwent excruciating treatment to mend his broken limbs. One leg was set so badly that a piece of bone was left sticking out. Ignatius didn't value his chances of winning a lady's hand with a misshapen leg and a limp, so he ordered further agonising treatment to try and re-set his bones. It never quite worked out and he had a pronounced limp for the rest of his life.

During his long convalescence on the top storey of his sister-in-law's house, the only reading material available, or so it seemed, was a copy of the Life of Christ and Lives of the Saints. There is some speculation that these are the only two books his sister-in-law Magdalena claimed were in the house, in a bid to restore her wayward brother-in-law to a life of virtue. At any rate, Ignatius spent his long immobile hours of recovery either reading these books or daydreaming about a heroic courtly career. He noticed something which unsettled him. When he thought of worldly success and glory, he felt briefly satisfied, but soon enough felt empty, or desolate. When he thought of a scene from the life of Christ or one of the saints, a life of sacrifice and holy endeavour working with the poorest of the poor, he felt a deeper consolation and a sense of peace and joy that seemed more solid than the transient dreams of courtly glory.

From this observation, Ignatius started to develop his teaching on the discernment of spirits. He understood that God was at work in our very feelings, in our imagination and desires. Also at work in us was what he called a bad spirit, working to draw us away from what was genuinely of God, tempting us to become attached to what is futile. Drawing on the teaching of St Augustine, Ignatius believed that we have an inner restlessness, a true desire, which only God can fulfil. The Creator has made his creatures with the equipment, if you like, to receive his signals and respond to him. We are "wired" for God, it's in our DNA to look for traces of this Creator in our everyday experience. Our life's work is to distinguish between those desires that lead away from God and the desire that deepens God's life in us.

By paying close attention to inner moods, Ignatius realised that he could begin to discern what God's Spirit was prompting him to do. In the smallest and most insignificant episodes and encounters of the day, Ignatius detected God at work in his imagination. In our age, we've become used to analysing the workings of our imagination, or the sub-conscious, but in the sixteenth century this was well ahead of its time. The theology that Ignatius was developing was that grace was at work in the ordinary, in our everyday lives. Grace was at work within us, prompting us to become the versions of ourselves that God had in mind when he made us, prompting us to use our gifts for the building up of the kingdom.

The great insights of St Ignatius have been taken up into the teaching of the Church. *Gaudium et Spes,* The Pastoral Constitution on the Church in the Modern World, states that "Christ is now at work in human hearts through the strength of his Spirit… animating, purifying and reinforcing the noble aspirations which drive the human family to make its life one that is more human."[(40)] In other words, the Spirit of God is at work beyond the walls of the church, in the hearts of all people. The same document also values the modern movements to promote the rights of humanity and the dignity of the person. This does not mean that the Church will agree with every aspect of popular movements, but where there are people working for racial justice, or freedom from harassment and abuse for women and girls, or for the care of the earth our common home, there the Spirit is at work. The great Jesuit theologian Karl Rahner expressed the work of grace in the ordinary in this way:

> When someone experiences laughter or tears, bears responsibility, stands by the truth, breaks through the egoism in his life with other people; when someone hopes against hope, faces the shallowness and stupidity of the daily rush and bustle with humour and patience, refusing to be embittered; when someone learns to be silent and in this inner silence lets the evil in his heart die rather than spread outward; in a word, whenever someone lives as he would like to live, combating his own egoism and the continual temptation to inner despair – there is an event of grace.[(41)]

The prayer that Ignatius developed for his brother Jesuits to help them discern the workings of the Holy Spirit in their daily life is known as the Examen. Every Jesuit, every day, devotes some time to this method of prayer. It is simple, like all good prayer, and like all prayer it is better when it is practised every day. There are a number of steps in the Examen. The first is to settle in God's presence and ask for the gift to see the day with God's merciful eyes and understanding. This might help us to keep a sense of perspective. Ignatius constantly reiterates the importance of gratitude as the bedrock of our relationship with God, so he invites us to review our day with a grateful heart. We try and recognise the gifts within the day: a quiet word, a simple meal, birdsong in the early morning. "The details may be small," says Sr Gemma Simmonds in *The Way of Ignatius*, "but God is to be found within them, thanked and praised."[(42)]

As we focus on events, we consider how they made us feel. What has provoked joy in us, or sadness? What gave us life, what drained it out of us? When did we fall short of the Gospel ideal? Where do we need to ask for healing, in all poverty and humility? We ask the Holy Spirit what we can learn from the day. We pray for God's grace and name whatever emerges as something or someone for which we want to pray, repent or thank God. Finally, we seek God's guidance for whatever lies ahead, praying in hope and sincerity. For Ignatius, the Examen is a very conversational prayer with a God who is very close to us and wants what is good for us, a God "who shines a compassionate and encouraging light on our daily reactions and interactions".[43] As a practical resource and part of our daily repertoire of prayer, I'd recommend the Examen. There is a long tradition in Christian spirituality of the **Examination of Conscience**. This may at times have dwelt too much on our sins, and not enough on what we should be grateful for, including God's Spirit active in our lives. The Examen is known as an **Examination of Consciousness**. Ten minutes at the end of every day praying the Examen is time well spent. At the end of the chapter, I've written an example of this prayer.

Contemplative prayer, a sharing between friends

One of the saints who is well known for writing about contemplative prayer is St Teresa of Avila, a sixteenth century Spanish mystic, who spent her adult life in the Carmelite order. She was a near contemporary of St Ignatius. Her most well-known book is *Interior Castle*, in which she describes the stages of the soul's journey through various "mansions" towards union with God. It was written for her sisters in the convent, in a very unpolished and accessible style. She doesn't have much time for the prima donnas of the spiritual life, who run themselves into ill health for the sake of piety. She is very grounded, because, like St Augustine, she believes that God is found within, not without.

Many of the themes we've covered on prayer feature in the *Interior Castle*. St Teresa talks about the importance of humility, "Without humility," she says, "all will be lost."[44] She makes it clear that thinking, or the faculty of reason, is not the best way to God. At the time, she may have been reacting to the medieval writers, who took reason and logic to extremes in their pursuit of truth. Teresa reminds us that "the important thing is not to think much, but to love much".[45] She does not see the need for elaborate prayer rituals, but believes that the soul can experience God directly, like water welling up in a fountain. This experience of God arises from the centre of the person. And as we've heard already, she is clear that there is not much we can do to acquire this great gift. "The person who does most," she says, "is he who thinks least."[46] She says that before God we are like beggars before an emperor. "The soul must just leave itself in the hands of God."[47] The *Catechism* quotes St Teresa's definition of contemplative prayer: "nothing else than a close sharing between friends; it means taking time frequently to be alone with him who we know loves us".[48]

The *Catechism* talks about contemplative prayer as abiding in "the dwelling place of the Lord".[49] We enter into the presence of the one who waits for us. We let our masks fall. We have nothing to bring but our poverty. "Contemplative prayer is the prayer of the child of God, of the forgiven sinner who agrees to welcome the love by which he or she is loved."[50] In this prayer, we sit in silence, in solitude and stillness, and open our hearts to the action and presence of the Holy Spirit dwelling in us. One of the methods of contemplative prayer which I have found most helpful is **Centering Prayer**, developed by monks in America in the 1970s to bring the tradition of Christian contemplation back into the mainstream life of the Church.

It is recommended that you devote two twenty minute sessions to Centering Prayer daily. This is easier said than done. I find twenty minutes in the morning not too difficult when the house is quiet, although when our children were young that would have meant getting up very early! In the evening I find it easier to find excuses (idolatry?) to avoid the session, but when I do manage to find a second twenty minutes it makes a difference. So, go to your "inner room" or a quiet space and sit straight on a chair, if your health permits. Compose yourself, be aware of your breathing, God's life in you. After a short prayer to the Holy Spirit, the method involves sitting still in silence with the intention to be open to the presence and action of the Trinity within us. Sounds dead easy, doesn't it?

But of course, within seconds, the "monkey mind" is at work, what the tradition calls *distractions*. When they come, and they will, as sure as day follows night, all the advice is not to do battle with them. Just come back to the intention to remain in prayerful encounter with the Lord by using a "sacred word" which is a personal choice. It should be short, perhaps "love" or "peace" and said just a few times to restore our silence. It is a symbol of our intention to be close to God. It is not a mantra; that is a different tradition of Christian meditation. The problem, as St Teresa said, is thinking, or the activity of the ego. When you think about it, most of our thinking is no great help in the spiritual life. Most of our thinking is repetitive, anxious, self-seeking, indulgent and obsessive (or maybe that's just me!). In silence, the *Catechism* reminds us, "The Father speaks to us his incarnate Word",[51] it is a communion of love, an attentiveness, a deep listening, an act of humility and devotion.

In the *Interior Castle*, St Teresa gives us an image which helps us to understand the difference between meditation and contemplation, or, in the terms we used in Chapter 4, between the phase of purgation and illumination. Teresa uses the image of a fountain, or rather two fountains, two basins of water.

In one the water comes to the basin over a long distance by means of conduits and human skill. This is the equivalent of meditation, using symbols, images, books, created things. It requires our thoughts and our effort, and it is tiring. It is also, as the water fills the basin, noisy.

The second image she uses is the basin which has been constructed at the very source of the water. No skill is necessary here, the water is flowing all the time. The water comes direct from its source, which is God, and "its coming is accompanied by the greatest peace and quietness and sweetness within ourselves".(52) St Teresa calls this the Prayer of Quiet, which requires no skill or thought or mental effort on our part, but comes directly from God as gift. All that's required from us is humility. The result of this experience is what Teresa calls a "dilation" or enlargement of the heart. Interestingly, she does not think that this happiness has its source in the heart at all, but from an even deeper part of ourselves, which she calls "our very depth".(53) The effect of this grace, the life of God within us, is to flood and enlarge our hearts, making us more open and generous and joyful, more like God.

I suspect that many of us who are on any kind of journey of Christian formation are somewhere on the border between the purgative and illuminative, between the active and the passive forms of prayer, between meditation and contemplation. You may of course be in the unitive stage, which corresponds to Teresa's final mansions, which is a kind of spiritual betrothal and is not without its suffering, what St Teresa's great contemporary St John of the Cross called the dark night of the soul. But all of the great spiritual teachers seem to say the same thing, that the journey proceeds from words and our own efforts, to fewer words, to silence, and a deep gratitude for the gift of God.

Action

We shouldn't think of St Teresa, or any of the other great mystics of the Church, as being some kind of detached introvert, with eyes only for heaven. Because she is rooted in scripture, she comes back time and again to the "two things" the Lord asks of us: love of God and love of neighbour. We cannot love one and not the other. "I do not believe we could ever attain perfect love for our neighbour unless it had its roots in the love of God."[54] She is critical of those in her community who act as if perfection in the spiritual life is only about prayer. "What the Lord desires is works",[55] she says, echoing the teaching of the Council of Trent, which had finished some 10 years before she wrote the *Interior Castle*.

In the Catholic tradition, salvation (or being justified, in right relation with God) is always about faith expressed in love for our neighbour, especially our most vulnerable neighbour, never just faith alone. Her version of love of neighbour is very much rooted in compassion, as in to *suffer with*. If you see a sick woman, she tells her sisters, take pity on her, but more than that, "if she is in pain, you should feel pain too; if necessary, fast so that she may have your food".[56] St Teresa links together the three great pillars of the Christian life: prayer, fasting and almsgiving.

Prayer, in the words of Pope Francis, "nourishes a daily commitment to love".[57] In the modern professional era, we are obsessed with impact and evaluation. Is our strategy and use of resources having an impact? The biblical language for this is "fruits". The fruit of authentic prayer is to be gradually transformed by grace, to undergo a liberating forgiveness, to forgive more readily in turn, to be more loving, more discerning of the most just way to live in our world. "Our worship becomes pleasing to God when we devote ourselves to living generously, and allow God's gift, granted in prayer, to be shown in our concern for our brothers and sisters."[58]

A day in the life

One spiritual practice which has been popular in recent years is **journaling**. It sounds like keeping a diary, but it's intended to be more reflective, with the focus on spiritual growth and the practices which help. It has been become associated with good mental health, especially in helping people deal with trauma.

It might be helpful to devote some time to a prayer journal, to record the devotional practices that work or didn't work so well and any other thoughts or insights that occur. It might be helpful to structure your day according to the advice of the *Didache*, which was to pray three times a day: in the morning, at midday, and in the evening.

What devotional prayers should be a feature of your day? If you're out of the habit of daily prayer, start with small steps and build up, perhaps a daily Examen, or rosary? The main thing is not to be discouraged. This is God's idea, not ours. He wants to meet us in prayer. All we have to do is turn up at the well with our empty jar.

Praying with Andrew

Faith and Light is a network of communities across the world made up of persons with an intellectual disability, their families and friends, who meet on a regular basis in a Christian spirit, to share friendship, pray together and celebrate life. I'm not sure why I went along to the meeting. Must have been the prompting of the Spirit. The first few times I felt very uncomfortable, singing children's songs and acting out simple scenarios. Then I got over myself and started to relax a bit and made friends with some people, in particular Andrew, who is about my age, a bit older, and has Down's syndrome.

I ended up a few weeks later taking Andrew to church on a Sunday morning, along with Fiona, another friend from his supported living complex, and her mother. I sat beside Andrew at Mass and was immediately impressed by his reverence. His speech isn't clear, but he knew when to respond. He started copying the gestures of the priest, raising his arms in prayer and so on. It turned out that Andrew, whose parents have both passed away, used to serve on the altar in our parish years ago. Sadly that stopped when one parish priest couldn't cope with Andrew on the altar. But we had a new parish priest and I asked him about Andrew serving on the altar again. He was very supportive and within a few weeks Andrew, and then Fiona, were serving on the altar. He was so proud of himself, carrying the cross in procession, ringing the bells, pouring the water over the priest's hands ever so carefully.

We started up a monthly lunch in the parish as another way to build social bonds and fraternity and also to break down social exclusion, especially among the elderly and many of our friends with intellectual disability. Andrew and Fiona helped to set up and serve the lunches and looked forward to the next one as soon as it was over. At the beginning of the lunch, our parish priest said grace before meals. One Sunday, Andrew got up and stood beside him, his eyes closed, his arms stretched out in prayer, ready for the grace before meals. Our parish priest, a wise and intuitive man, turned to Andrew and said, "Why don't you say the prayer, Andrew?" Andrew opened his eyes. His face lit up and he smiled. "All right then, I will!" He gathered himself up, took a deep breath and prayed. Most of the words we couldn't make out, but it was prayer all right. It was a prayer of the heart; it was the Holy Spirit praying in Andrew. No need for many clever words anyway, Jesus made that very clear.

So after all that *Catechism*, all that thinking, I think my best lesson in prayer has been from Andrew, my friend, a person the world might regard as useless, unproductive, a burden. A person that in many cultures would not be allowed to be born for those reasons, because in the eyes of some he is not fully or properly a human being. But he is a child of God, capable of loving and being loved, and it is the pure in heart who are closest to God. He taught me how to pray with reverence, sincerity, and humility.

HOW

Practical resources for growing in faith through prayer

Examen. There are many good websites run by the Jesuits which offer advice and guidance on the Examen and the other riches of Ignatian spirituality, such as: https://www.ignatianspirituality.com/ignatian-prayer/the-examen/

Reimagining the Examen, by Mark E. Thibodeaux SJ. A collection of Examen prayers to help expand your understanding of the prayer, with various themes.

Centering Prayer. Contemplative Outreach was founded by Fr Thomas Keating, one of the figures behind the development of Centering Prayer. The website includes videos of Fr Keating's talks: https://www.contemplativeoutreach.org/

The Catholic Prayer Book, by Tony Castle (ed.). A treasure box of traditional prayers, quotations from the saints, a guide to the rosary, and to other types of devotional prayer such as the Stations of the Cross.

YOUCAT. A beautiful collection of prayers designed for young people, ideal for use in schools and university chaplaincy, but suitable for any age or community.

At Your Side, by Raymond Friel and David Wells. At the risk of blowing my own trumpet, a collection of original prayers inspired by the very ordinary events of life. Besides, all the best ones are by David Wells.

Prayers for a Privileged People, by Walter Brueggemann. Powerful original prayers with a focus on social justice.

Prayer Seeds, by Joyce Rupp. A beautiful collection of blessings, reflections and poems for spiritual growth.

Learning to Pray, by James Martin SJ. A comprehensive survey of the various traditions and types of prayer.

Prayer: Our Deepest Longing, by Ronald Rolheiser. Excellent on the difference between devotional and liturgical, or priestly, prayer.

Examen

Lord, as the day comes to an end
help me to settle for a moment in your presence,
to be still and know
that you are God, to let go
of the cares and anxieties for a while,
to be grateful for my life,
for the blessings I take for granted,
for the gift of everything.

Spirit of God,
walk with me through this day.
Help me to understand
when you were speaking to me –
in my encounters with people, my thoughts, my moods,
my quickening, my darkening;
my reactions to unexpected moments, to interruptions.
Bid me pause at the stations of simplicity,

the graced moments
of the everyday.

What rises in me when I think of today?
What plays on my mind? What tugs at my heart?
What drained me of life? What enlivened me?
What stretched me a little into being?
  What diminished me?

What did I do for others
that was helpful, that was unhelpful?
When did I show love, when was love shown to me?
Where might I have been more attentive?
What in my lifestyle remains unexamined
that I know is unhealthy, selfish, unsustainable?
What am I sorry for?
Help me to name the grace I need.

Where do you need to get at me, Lord,
to make me more forgiving, more compassionate,
    more patient,
more committed to my neighbour,
    especially the vulnerable ones?
Lord, as we journey on together,
    keep me free from fear and anxiety,
show me how I can grow, can change for the better,
give me a heart for the way ahead.

Chapter SEVEN References

1. CCC, 2657
2. Ronald Rolheiser, *Prayer: Our Deepest Longing* (Cincinnati: Franciscan Media, 2013), 27
3. CCC, 2656
4. Pope Francis, *Fratelli Tutti*, title of Chapter 4
5. CCC, 2562
6. CCC, 2563
7. CCC, 2565
8. CCC, 2699
9. CCC, 2559
10. CCC, 2560
11. CCC, 2559
12. *Deus Caritas Est*, 36
13. *Deus Caritas Est*, 36
14. *Deus Caritas Est*, 37
15. *Deus Caritas Est*, 37
16. CCC, 2697
17. CCC, 2700
18. CCC, 2629
19. *Gaudete et Exsultate*, 154
20. Denis McBride, C.Ss.R., *At Your Side*, by Raymond Friel and David Wells (Chawton: Redemptorist Publications, 2020), Foreword
21. Elie Wiesel, *Night* (London: Penguin Books, 1985), 64-65
22. Lawrence Kushner, *God Was In This Place And I, I did not know* (Woodstock: Jewish Lights Publishing, 2016), 55
23. Kushner, 55
24. CCC, 310
25. Kushner, 57
26. CCC, 312
27. CCC, 1708

28. CCC, 2606
29. CCC, 2606
30. Second Vatican Council, *Lumen Gentium* (Dogmatic Constitution on the Church), 39
31. *Gaudete et Exsultate*, 20
32. *Gaudete et Exsultate*, 14
33. *Gaudete et Exsultate*, 147
34. *Gaudete et Exsultate*, 29
35. CCC, 2705
36. CCC, 2708
37. CCC, 2706
38. CCC, 2706
39. CCC, 2706
40. *Gaudium et Spes*, 38
41. Karl Rahner, "Secular Life and the Sacraments: a Copernican revolution", *The Tablet* (6 & 13 March 1971)
42. Gemma Simmonds, CJ, *The Way of Ignatius: A Prayer Journey through Lent* (London: SPCK, 2018), 13
43. Gemma Simmonds, CJ, 14
44. St Teresa of Avila, *Interior Castle* (New York: Dover Publications, 2007), 23
45. St Teresa of Avila, 49
46. St Teresa of Avila, 58
47. St Teresa of Avila, 59
48. CCC, 2709
49. CCC, 2711
50. CCC, 2712
51. CCC, 2717
52. St Teresa of Avila, 53
53. St Teresa of Avila, 54
54. St Teresa of Avila, 78
55. St Teresa of Avila, 80
56. St Teresa of Avila, 80
57. *Gaudete et Exsultate*, 104
58. *Gaudete et Exsultate*, 104

Commitment to a life of virtue, "Do you see this woman?"

In the final chapter I'd like to consider what a life looks like which is committed to the kingdom of God. How do we as Catholic Christians see, discern and act in the world in a way which is consistent with the Gospel? Not all the situations we might face in our lives are covered in sacred scripture. We have a range of choices, temptations and moral complexity which is arguably greater than that faced by previous generations. Since the 1950s, in the west, we have lived in what has been called the "great acceleration" – the most remarkable growth in economic activity and wealth ever seen in human history. After the Second World War, there was a step change in economic growth, the use of energy, expansion of personal transport, construction projects, development of consumer goods, telecommunication and international tourism, to name but a few. The benefits have not been evenly shared, people and places have been left behind, and the impact on the natural world has been immense. We have seen dramatic changes to the level of CO_2 emissions, to stratospheric ozone, loss of forests, the increase in coastal nitrogen and ocean acidification. Creation is on the brink of permanent damage. Some call this freedom, for others it is the worst of the human condition on steroids.

Some good has come out of this era: a compelling expression of universal human rights, progress in civil and minority rights, extended education, healthcare and social mobility.

Many have been lifted out of poverty and offered a standard of living which was unimaginable to our predecessors. However, some underlying trends are more ominous: the fabric of local community has been shredded by economic growth and globalisation; the winners in this world are "fortified" in castles of protection, the ones who run the basic services to keep all this going are increasingly harassed, run by algorithms, one "strike" away from being cast side. The great acceleration of the 1950s put on the booster rockets of neoliberal economics in the 1980s. Any early concerns about the environment in the 1960s and 70s were drowned out; money was king. In the infamous phrase of one political leader, "there is no such thing as society". The great vision sold to the people was that this was freedom, a freedom based on relentless increases in GDP, consumer choice and material gain. Freedom as the "right to choose" – whether that is the choice of consumer goods, or what to do with your own body.

Choice, of course, depends on your resources. The ability to choose is determined by competition. The "successful" are those who can access the goods of the market, who have power over others, who make profit. The "losers" are left behind, unseen, excluded, their voices muted, their stories unheard. They also need to be kept out. Violence is necessary to maintain this culture – structural, physical, relational violence – since not everyone can consume to the same extent. The planet could not cope. It is the culture, the cult, of the individual achiever. The culture of the commodification of human beings and nature in the service of the market. The culture of eros, not agape; contract, not covenant; ownership, not stewardship; a culture that undermines community and the common good, that leads to the kind of alienation we saw in Luke's Gospel with the man who built bigger barns and ended up talking to himself. A culture that "sees" the world through the lens of greed and personal power. Don Draper was the main character in the American hit TV series, *Mad Men*, about the advertising industry in New York in the 1950s and 60s. One of his most memorable lines summed up the era: "Happiness is the smell of a new car". For those who can afford a new car.

What chance does the Gospel of community, humility, poverty, forgiveness and service have in a culture that idolises individual achievement, status, possessions, pleasure, winning and power? What chance does a message of freedom as dying to self and love of enemies have against a message of freedom as doing what you want? What chance does a Christian have to live a Christian life when they are "enculturated" in such a society? What has the most influence on our operative values, being brought up as a Catholic, or brought up as a member of this society? To paraphrase a well-known mantra from the business schools, *Does culture eat religion for breakfast*? Do Catholic Christians stand out in this culture because they live differently, turning their backs on the lure of wealth and hedonism? Or do they live more or less like everybody else in their socio-economic group, but just hold different beliefs and go to religious services? Pope Francis has been uncompromising about the culture of consumerism:

> The great danger in today's world, pervaded as it is by consumerism, is the desolation and anguish born of a complacent yet covetous heart, the feverish pursuit of frivolous pleasures, and a blunted conscience. Whenever our interior life becomes caught up in its own interests and concerns, there is no longer room for others, no place for the poor.[(1)]

A covetous heart is one which desires the treasures of this world, the treasures of others. The tenth commandment forbade the coveting of what belonged to our neighbour. This kind of imitative desire seems to be a part of the human condition. Limits were set to enable human flourishing in God's eyes. In Chapter 1, we mentioned the French theologian and anthropologist René Girard whose key teaching is that *we desire according to the desire of the other*. I think there is ancient wisdom in that insight. It needed a commandment to hold it in check. It is what the advertising industry is built on, what Don Draper manipulated with cunning skill. I didn't know I wanted that until I saw this beautiful one on television, or my neighbour wearing it, or driving it, or living in it. I will be a lesser person until I have it. This even applies to people, the body as an object of desire which the pornography industry thrives on. As noted in Chapter 1, this desire is insatiable, we will literally never be satisfied, since someone will always have more than me. So the culture of desire breeds the culture of anxiety: about my status, my body, my car. It is a "rest-less" culture. Even holidays just become another expression of desire and competition, an exhausting pursuit of pleasure and stimulation. It is the "grasping" of the Garden of Eden, the primordial sin, a turning in to our own desires rather than a looking out for the needs of others.

It's important to say as well that humanity is always a mixed blessing. It's not a relentlessly bleak picture. The Holy Spirit is at work in human hearts and grace is breaking through everywhere. We have created a culture of desire like no other in human history, but we must not lose sight of the goodness in people, the love that keeps challenging the selfishness by its very presence. In the "exile" of lockdown we saw an eruption of fraternity: many volunteering to help vulnerable neighbours, expressions of gratitude for those who perform essential services with such dignity and diligence, public discussion of the common good and building back better. The insight of the Christian tradition is that human beings are flawed, prone to sin, so for every outbreak of fraternity we'll see the drag back into old self-serving ways. No sooner had lockdown finished than we saw signs in shops and restaurants about being kind to the staff because they were on the frontline of pent-up aggression and frustration. Always a mixed blessing.

We must keep asking ourselves how we can hold on to the best version of humanity which, for the Christian, is humanity empowered by the grace of the Holy Spirit. We must keep asking how is it possible to live in this culture in a way which is authentically Christian, following the way of the cross we have looked at in previous chapters, seeing the fruits of creation as gifts for all, rather than products for some? To live in a way which regards all human beings as possessing the inherent dignity of images of God, rather than regarding some as more important than others, while the harassment and degradation of others are just inevitable consequences of the rat race? These are not easy questions to deal with and anyone who presumes to offer any insights needs to be aware of their own complicity with this culture.

Nevertheless, I think it's important that we try to bring as much honesty to this as possible, or else our Catholicism will be no more than a cultural habit which has little impact on our operative values and choices. I'm suggesting here that the key to living in this culture in a way which is authentically Christian is virtue, inspired by grace, and the starting point for virtue is to develop a heart which sees as God sees, not a heart which is clouded by the culture of desire and anxiety. Our own moral lives I believe are determined by our seeing.

Our seeing is determined by the state of our hearts, the seat of desire and choosing. If we see the world as essentially there to serve my needs and desires, then we see opportunities or obstacles. If we see the world through God's eyes – the whole point of our formation – then we see with compassion and we see where we might be able to exercise charity, promote justice, or restore dignity.

Dear prudence

To exercise Christian charity, or compassion, in the situations we face in life, or in the decisions we make, requires judgement, or in the Ignatian term favoured by Pope Francis, *discernment*. The purpose of our formation is the dilation of our heart so that it "sees" as Christ sees the world and is prompted by the Holy Spirit to act in the best way to cooperate with the Father's plan for the new creation. The traditional formulation is that God creates (Father), redeems (Son) and sanctifies (Holy Spirit) the world, ahead of its consummation in heaven. We participate in the sanctification (making holy) of the world by offering ourselves up in service and working for a world in which our brothers and sisters can live a more fully human life. This is happiness for the Christian, not the smell of a new car. The path of this sanctification is the path of virtue.

Being virtuous should not be confused with the idea of living a somehow faultless life with overtones of "holier than thou" (I know I'm virtuous because you're vicious!). Being virtuous, or being committed to a life of virtue, has deep roots in scripture and the tradition. We'll start with what are sometimes called the human virtues, or the cardinal virtues (from the Latin for "hinge", as in pivotal). In the Wisdom of Solomon, we find the first reference to what became known as the cardinal virtues: "And if anyone loves righteousness, her labours are virtues; for she teaches self-control and prudence, justice and courage; nothing in life is more profitable for mortals than these" (Wisdom of Solomon 8:7).

A virtue is "an habitual and firm disposition to do the good".[2] Virtues are learned and habitual, they grow by being done and reflected on over time. The human virtues are acquired by human effort, but I'm not sure that's the whole story. The *Catechism* does say that the practice of virtue forges character, "with God's help".[3] It is not easy for us to stay on the path of virtue since we are "wounded" by sin, inclined to selfishness and to look for happiness in the wrong places, which is why "Christ's gift of salvation offers us the grace necessary to persevere in the pursuit of the virtues."[4] To say that the pursuit of virtue is entirely down to our efforts sounds like the Pelagianism we looked at in Chapter 6. We'll have a look at the human virtues and how they help us to see and act in a Christian way in the complexities of this life, entangled as we are in the culture of desire; residents in the empire of things. Let's start with prudence.

Prudence is often misunderstood in English as a kind of risk-free attitude to life. The prudent person is cautious, unromantic, controlled. This is not the meaning of prudence in the Christian tradition. Prudence is regarded as the lead human virtue, what the *Catechism* poetically calls the "charioteer of the virtues",[5] the one that drives the others. The definition of St Thomas Aquinas is hard to beat as a succinct definition of prudence, "right reason in action".[6] Prudence guides the judgement of conscience, gathers in all the relevant factors in any situation or decision and arrives at a decision about "the good to achieve and the evil to avoid".[7] At the beginning of the twentieth century, a Belgian priest,

Fr Joseph Cardijn, used the teaching of Aquinas on prudence as the basis for the See-Judge-Act methodology he developed for the Young Christian Worker movement. Cardijn went on to become a Cardinal and the influence of his See-Judge-Act methodology was enshrined in magisterial teaching by St Pope John XXIII in his 1961 encyclical, *Mater et Magistra*:

> There are three stages which should normally be followed in the reduction of social principles into practice. First, one reviews the concrete situation; secondly, one forms a judgment on it in the light of these same principles; thirdly, one decides what in the circumstances can and should be done to implement these principles. These are the three stages that are usually expressed in the three terms: look, judge, act.[8]

The life of grace which grows in us through faith, through the practices we have explored in the previous chapters, insists on acting in the world for the common good. Christianity is a doing religion. Karl Marx's famous jibe about religion as an opium which kept the people quiet was wide of the mark. Christianity is a stimulus to action. The See-Judge-Act method gives us the tools to act in the way most in conformity with the Gospel and the teaching of the Church. After Vatican II, the method disappeared somewhat from the mainstream of Catholic life, at least in the northern hemisphere. It was a mainstay of liberation theology in South America. It was from there that Pope Francis brought the method back to the attention of the Church.

In his book-length interview with Austen Ivereigh, *Let Us Dream*, Pope Francis gives us an excellent summary of the method. It can be used in relation to our own moral choices, "What do I see, how can I discern in the light of faith, what should I do?" The Examen is just as well suited for that kind of personal reflection, perhaps more so. The practice of See-Judge-

Act, while it trains the individual in the virtue of prudence, also works effectively as group discernment, which of course will influence individual moral choices, but will also help to form a community approach to the common good. We can consider the pressing questions of our day, for example where is injustice in our community, how do we respond to migrating persons coming to our country, where is there racism and sexism in our community, do we take the climate crisis seriously? It can help a parish consider how it might renew its mission and engage with its local community. It can help a school consider how it might be more true to its values. It is training for our seeing, it is formation in how compassion should be enacted with justice in various circumstances. It can become the habitual way that we consider any situation and what the Gospel response should be. As the bumper sticker used to say: *What Would Jesus Do*?

Do you see this woman?

Let's take a break from the theory and go back to scripture, where we should frequently go to see how a human being should behave in this world. Jesus was without sin, he showed us what it was like to be truly human, to live according to love. Our understanding of See-Judge-Act will be enriched by looking at an example of how Jesus sees. Our seeing, unlike his, is clouded by original sin. Our seeing is distorted by concupiscence. We look for what will bring us pleasure. We look through the lens of rigid ideologies. We look through the lens of rivalry and envy: am I stronger, or funnier, or better looking than this one? Only grace can cleanse our seeing, wipe the lens clean. In Chapter 7 of Luke's Gospel there is a beautiful scene, which is all about seeing. Jesus is invited to dinner at the house of Simon the Pharisee. Jesus has already had run-ins with the Pharisees over the forgiveness of sins (Luke 5:21) and plucking grain on the Sabbath (Luke 6:2), so the atmosphere around the dinner was not friendly. This is confirmed later in the passage when it's revealed that Simon breached the cultural norms of hospitality by not offering Jesus a kiss of welcome or washing his dusty feet. Today, although our cultural norms around hospitality are not as strong, it might be like inviting someone to your home and when they arrive not taking their coat, or offering them a drink, and keeping the TV on. It is remarkably bad manners and can only have had one intention: to humiliate Jesus. It looks like another trap, a way to deal with this new teacher who is something of a threat to the legalistic world view of the Pharisees.

Into this tense scene comes an unnamed woman, "who was a sinner" (7:37), although the reason she was considered a sinner is not mentioned. Like Mary Magdalene, the assumption has often been that she was a prostitute, but there were many reasons at the time why a woman might have been considered a sinner, including simply working with Gentiles. She brings with her an alabaster jar of ointment, an expensive perfume, and in a scene of remarkable intimacy in front of the other guests, she weeps and kisses the feet of Jesus as he reclines at table, drying them with her hair. In a dinner of this kind, the guests would have reclined on sofas or cushions on their left side around a three-sided arrangement of tables, just as the disciples did at the Last Supper (remember the Beloved Disciple leaning into Jesus). So the woman has access to the feet of Jesus as he reclines, she's not under the table.

Simon the host "saw it" (7:39) but doesn't say anything. Luke, however, tells us what he was thinking. He has come to two conclusions: about the "kind of woman" (7:39) this woman is and that Jesus, by tolerating this intimacy from a sinner, is no prophet. Jesus sees through his judgements. He is an extraordinarily acute observer of human beings. He sees the heart. He also knows how to make a point. Instead of going for the direct confrontation, he tells Simon a short parable. This will take root in his imagination more readily than an argument. Who will love a forgiving creditor more, the one with the large debt or the small debt? "I suppose the one for whom he cancelled the greater debt" (7:43), said Simon. You're right, Jesus tells him, then in a remarkable moment he looks at the woman, but speaks to Simon. "Do you see this woman?" (7:44). What Simon "sees" is not a woman but a sinner, unworthy of his regard. He does not even speak to her. Then Jesus tells him what he sees.

She is the one who has offered the hospitality which the host has failed to do. She has kissed and washed the feet of Jesus with ointment and tears, dried them with her hair. Why? Because her sins have been forgiven. Her great love is the result of her forgiveness. Some translations make it sound as if she is forgiven because of her lavish demonstration of love (as if she could "earn" forgiveness), but most scholars now seem to agree that the tense of the Greek verb *"apheontai"* (have been forgiven) indicates an event which has already happened. They have met before, she has been "let go" of her sins, "hence she has shown great love" (Luke 7:47). Her coming to new life has passed through forgiveness. Her heart has been broken open and expanded into a life she did not know was possible. Hence the depth of her gratitude and love towards Jesus. She is a forgiven one who has been offered new life. Jesus does not take credit for these moments of conversion. He is so magnanimous. He does what Simon doesn't, he speaks to the woman. He says to her, "your faith has saved you; go in peace" (7:50). She has been saved by grace (forgiveness), through faith, shown in love. As Pope

Francis said, Jesus "anoints her with dignity".[9] He restores dignity and value to human beings. He sees them as children of God, he sees with God's eyes and "God saw everything that he had made, and indeed, it was very good" (Genesis 1:31).

After that, does Simon see any differently? We don't know, we don't hear any more from him. Luke the master storyteller invites our imagination to consider the look on Simon's face when he listens to Jesus. The fact that "those who were at table" (7:49) react by muttering among themselves about what right Jesus had to forgive sins, suggests that he and his group are unchanged. He is locked into a way of seeing determined by his ideology. Between himself and the woman there is a world of right and wrong which reduces human beings to categories, and it's easy enough to condemn a category. Jesus invites us to a much wider and more generous seeing. This woman isn't someone forever trapped in condemnation, but a forgiven child of God. How do we "see" when we look at people? How do we see ourselves in relation to them? What "filters" determine our looking? As Pope Francis has said, do we see an adjective, or a noun? Do we see a label, or the rich complexity and reality of a human being whom we can get to know by personal encounter, not dismiss by inherited prejudice or ideology?

To get to know how we see is uncomfortable work. To see through the filters of our upbringing, our mimetic desires, our assumptions about gender, race, other nationalities, whatever it is, is a painful part of conversion, but necessary if we are to see our fellow human beings with the compassionate eyes of Jesus. We are not just re-training our vision of the other but learning to see what lies between us and the other, in other words the relationship between us. Where is the power in this relationship? Does one have authority over the other, does one have a voice, the other not? What motivates our approach to this relationship? Is it the desire to "have" in some way, psychologically or physically, or the desire to ignore and humiliate and thereby reinforce my view of myself and my group? The Gospel calls upon us to transform and renew relationships, to restore and build community.

The inconvenient truth is that a community of relationships based on love has no room for domination, or the ownership or degradation of people. As St Paul said, "there is no longer slave or free" (Galatians 3:28) – social distinctions are of the kingdom of this world. The kingdom of God does not regard people as functions of an ideology (religious or secular), as commodities in the marketplace, to be used to produce goods, or indeed to be the goods, to be bought and sold for profit. The community we glimpsed in the early days of Christianity, and which keeps re-appearing at different points in history, is the community of the kingdom of God, the fellowship of those who owned all things in common. The tender community of the forgiven ones.

We might find something close to that original community in a religious order, where everyone lives together owning everything in common, where everyone has made vows of poverty, as well as chastity and obedience, depending on the order. But most Catholics live in the same street, the same town, as everybody else. There has been some interest recently in the creation of Catholic enclaves, the "Catholic village", but for most that's not an option, and I'm not sure it's all that healthy. Lay people are called to live in the world and be the "leaven" of the Gospel. We're called to a lifestyle and personal choices which are consistent with the Gospel. The level of intentional poverty we adopt, the way we behave in our relationships: these are not dictated in a modern day *Didache* for us. It is a matter of conscience and discernment.

We have our Teacher, his presence in sacred scripture and in the liturgy, and the social doctrine of the Church, to form our seeing and to guide our decision-making.

Prudence, otherwise known as See-Judge-Act

The first step is to see reality as clearly as possible for what it is, to come close to reality, to be moved by it, to ask why things are as they are. This is not a desktop exercise, nor is it straightforward, since what one person sees as significant, another sees as insignificant. Our "seeing", as we've noted, is formed by our upbringing, our cultural influences, our religion, our politics, our personality, but as we grow and mature as Christian disciples, our seeing needs to be more and more formed by the Gospel and the teaching of the Church. Pope Francis begins his seeing with an overview of the economic and political system which has been exposed as a failure in the pandemic. He proposes that at the root of the problem is a throwaway culture, a culture of selfishness which sees the earth as there to be plundered, and others as there to meet our needs; the mindset that what we have earned and achieved we deserve, even if that is at the expense of others. At the heart of this culture is another virus, the virus of indifference.

Lockdown made visible those who were invisible, the ones we rely on for the goods and services that keep us alive: the delivery drivers, the cleaners, the shop assistants, the rubbish collectors, the warehouse workers. These are often among what has come to be called the "precariat" – those whose jobs are insecure and who struggle on a low income. There was also a focus on the destitute, the rough sleepers, who were all offered a bed in the "Everybody In" initiative.

We thought of those who lived on their own, often in poor health, and who had little human contact. As we came through the pandemic, these people somewhat faded back into invisibility; the "new normal" looks much like the old normal. Pope Francis wants us to stay focused on the margins, the precarious and forgotten ones. He says, "You have to go to the edges of existence if you want to see the world as it is."[(10)] We don't have a good view of the world from a comfortable position, and this applies to the Church as well, especially in middle-class settings. If we're among those who are untroubled by poverty and exploitation, then any "solutions" we come up with for a better Church or world may fall into the trap of not shaking the status quo. The world looks clearer from the periphery, says Francis.

The Pope roots this approach in revelation itself. He says that when God wanted to regenerate creation, he chose to go to the margins, to announce the liberation of the oppressed – to places of sin and misery, of exclusion and suffering, of illness and solitude. The road to the margins is the route of the Incarnation. "God chose the peripheries as the place to reveal, in Jesus, His saving action in history."[(11)] Jesus "emptied himself" (Philippians 2:7) to assume the condition of a slave, as St Paul reminds us in one of the earliest texts in the New Testament, the letter to the Philippians. He did not live among the elite in Jerusalem, debating the finer points of the law. He lived on the margins, in Galilee, in the hand-to-mouth village of Nazareth, involved in manual work. In his ministry, he spent his time on the road, with nowhere to lay his head (Luke 9:58), among the poor and excluded, bringing to them the dignity of being loved and valued.

The religion of Jesus' day was, in the words of Francis, imprisoned in "the confines of the elite, of specialized knowledge and of privileged families".[12] By being "in charge" of religion, the elites could put themselves above others, those not like them, whom they inspected and judged. Jesus very quickly ran into conflict with this mindset because he challenged it, he subverted it. "By walking with the poor, the outcasts and the marginalized, he smashed the wall that prevented the Lord from coming close to His people, among his flock."[13] Jesus restored the true worth of the downtrodden, the ones for whom the authorities acted as "gatekeepers" to God and all things holy. He touched them, talked to them, healed them, invited them to the banquet.

He liberated them. Not by means of violent social revolution – Jesus was not Spartacus, as Pope Benedict XVI said, but in the sense of liberating them from the burden of sin imposed by the law and its mediators, liberating them from exclusion, restoring them to dignity and belonging. He awoke in them an ancient awareness of the closeness of God. He brought God's forgiveness to human hearts. No wonder they killed him. He posed a threat to any society based on less than love. As the Dominican Herbert McCabe said, "Jesus posed a political threat not by being a politician but by making people secure, by creating a kind of relationship that couldn't be accommodated within a society ultimately based on domination and fear."[14]

The Church was born, as Pope Francis says, "in the margins of the Cross where so many of the crucified are found".[15] He goes on to say that "if the church disowns the poor, she ceases to be the Church of Jesus; she falls back on the old temptation to become a moral or intellectual elite".[16] The mission of the Church, according to Herbert McCabe, is "the establishment of a new human race, of a society in which there is no fear, in which the bonds between people are bonds of love".[17] In this kingdom of God, we do not need to look to the gods or any ideology for meaning. Jesus is alive and with us and his Spirit is guiding us into all truth (John 16:13). His love is among us. We do not need to look to a corrupt and exploitative society for belonging and purpose. Although original sin is still all around us, it does not enslave us, we are free. We are sent to bring this good news to all the nations, beginning at the periphery, where Jesus began, where we will find him in the sick, the hungry, the naked (Matthew 25:34-36).

In order to see clearly we must go to the edges, the periphery, wherever that might be in the community we serve. Who is on the periphery, whose voices are seldom heard, whose voices are muted, who are the enslaved and indebted ones? It is skilled work to see through our own seeing so that the ones on the margins are not just heard, or helped, but become the protagonists of change. This is an important point. It is not just a case of helping this group or that with what we think they need. It is about giving people value, worth and agency. It's about empathy, about drawing close, getting alongside people. This means that we are not necessarily the ones who should even be framing the questions. Who can tell us what else we need to "see", what other "data" do we need to gather to provide ourselves with a full picture of our reality? Above all, keep asking why is this the case? These are all the questions that need to be considered to conduct a process of seeing that does not fall prey to the vested interests of those at or near the centre.

The next step is to discern what is of God and what is seeking to frustrate His will. Pope Francis urges us to resist the temptation of the immediate or hasty decision, to be willing to hold different options before the Lord. We need to consider reasons for and against an option, knowing that Jesus is with us and for us. We feel inside ourselves what he calls "the gentle pull of the Spirit"[18] and its opposite, the more strident and insistent pull of what he calls the "bad spirit". We need a refuge from the tyranny of the urgent. If we are to read the signs of the times, the signs of our community, the signs of our own life, we need to make time for silent reflection, for prayer, for dialogue. We need to be open to reality. We need a set of principles, or criteria, drawn from the Gospels, from the "grammar of the kingdom of God".[19] We have been calling these principles Catholic Social Teaching, sometimes referred to as the Church's social doctrine, which "proposes principles for reflection; it provides criteria for judgement; it gives guidelines for action".[20]

Pope Francis reminds us that the heart of this teaching is about "expressions of love" – *Caritas* – "that allow people to feel loved, especially the poor, who are able to experience their true value".[21] In *Let Us Dream*, Pope Francis concentrates on the main principles in Catholic Social Teaching: the dignity of the person, leading us to the preferential option for the poor; the common good; the universal destination of goods; solidarity and subsidiarity. The preferential option for the poor, which runs throughout scripture, but has found specific expression in the Church in recent years, is inspired by the foundational belief in the dignity of all human beings. For Francis, it means that we must always "keep in mind how any decisions we make might impact the poor".[22] It means putting the poor at the centre of our thinking and, as we've noted before, making it possible for them to be protagonists in the conversation, not just the grateful recipients of our charity. This preferential option opens up a new perspective, a Gospel perspective, a Jesus perspective if you like, with which to judge or discern events. It also means considering the different kinds of poverty, the various ways people experience oppressive situations. It could be material deprivation, but it could also be social isolation, trauma, the stress of debt, domestic abuse, addiction, victimisation.

When the Pope speaks about the common good, this means the need to have regard for society as a whole. It's not enough to adjudicate between competing interests and work towards a solution based on the greatest happiness of the greatest number. That's the nineteenth century concept of utilitarianism and is not the same as the common good. In a utilitarian solution, the interests of the majority hold sway, which means that the needs of the minority are neglected. The common good invites us all to consider what is the "good" we seek, what it is that we are worthy of as a society. The Church has a distinctive contribution to make to this debate when it says that the "good" we seek is not based on the anxiety of consumerism, or the drive to dominate and exploit others, but a society based on the bonds of love where no one is subject to dehumanising conditions or is consigned to the category of shamed outcast, where all can flourish and take responsibility and participate.

Solidarity acknowledges our interconnectedness. We are creatures in relationship, one family with the same basic DNA, a truth enshrined in the biblical account of creation which described our ancestry in the same parents. Solidarity is always in danger of being reduced to a slogan, a kind of "We Are the World" feel-good moment. Solidarity is more than just saying we are all one. It comes with duties towards each other, working towards the transformation of the systems which consign people to poverty. It means "welcoming the stranger, forgiving debts, giving a home to the disabled, and allowing other people's dreams and hopes for a better life to become our own".[23] It means creating *structures of solidarity* at the most local level to undermine and supplant the *structures of sin*. This takes us on to subsidiarity.

Subsidiarity ensures that we respect "the autonomy of others as subjects of their own destiny".[24] Decisions should not be taken at a higher level if the same decisions can be taken closer to the people who will feel their impact. In practice, this is a real challenge, and it is easier to ignore it and settle for default decision-making habits. But when it starts to get a hold in a community, it can make a real difference. It is the basis for many new movements in society towards localism, community organising, de-centralised institutions and funding. The poor are not the objects of our pity and good intentions but the protagonists of their own future, imbued with the same dignity as every other person on this earth.

The final step, having taken our time to discern what is of God and what is not, what will promote human dignity and what will not, having opened up the space to listen to God's Spirit, to recognise in prayer God's invitations and prompts, is to decide what needs to be done to heal and repair, to make the community, the parish, the school, more conformed to the "gospel of God" (Romans 1:1), the good news that God loves us and wants to free us from all oppressive situations. What actions will be most likely to bring about the right kind of change? What opposition do we anticipate? Do we have the resources to act in the way we want to, if not what do we do about that? It's also an opportunity to think boldly about leadership and positions of responsibility. Do we need a whole new approach? Are there people whose time has now come, who might step up and offer fresh energy and a new perspective? It's an opportunity to break out of old habits of thinking.

And with any plan of action, we should build in plenty of time to review its fruits. Can we be honest when looking at what we've done? Was it the right thing to do, were the right people doing the right things? How do we know it was of God at all? Well, look at the fruits. If it has brought about any increase in the fruits of the Spirit – "love, joy, peace, patience, kindness, generosity, faithfulness, gentleness, and self-control" (Galatians 5:22) – then it is likely to be of God. If it has brought about the opposite, then it's not a path to continue on, although we should always remember that God's plans will be met with noisy opposition. The process is cyclical and the more it is practised, the more each part is developed. For example, the more that the Gospel and Catholic Social Teaching are discerned, the more the question "why is this the case?" will be informed bythe Gospel.

One final point on See-Judge-Act needs a brief mention. In many conversations with people about the method, one question keeps coming up: what if, after careful discernment by a group, there are several proposals for how to act, all apparently rooted in the Gospel and Catholic Social Teaching? It is entirely possible. The temptation is to operate an authority structure in which one person (too often in Catholic groups the priest) makes the final call. Well, that's one way to achieve a tidy outcome, but it might be better to hang in there, to keep praying and discerning, until a course of action presents itself. The Ignatian tradition tells us that the process of making good decisions is seldom between a good and an evil choice, but between two goods, so it's coming to an understanding of the better good, or "the more" (Latin: *magis*). What shouldn't really be difficult is to know what you see when you see a human being. The person who stumbles out of a dinghy onto a beach in Kent is, in the eyes of God and the teaching of the Church, a human being of exceptional dignity. Not a threat, or a scrounger, or whatever other emotive label some people wish to apply. This is a child of God, deserving of dignity and a truly human life. To argue otherwise seems to me to have left the discourse of the Church.

For the path to a better future, Pope Francis suggests some key concepts that should guide our actions. He says that what the Lord asks of us today is a culture of service, not a throwaway culture. He calls for a solidarity that can harness the "eruption of fraternity"[25] we saw in lockdown, when neighbour reached out to neighbour, especially the vulnerable neighbour. He calls for an end to the globalisation of indifference and the cult of the individual. We need to feel again that we belong to each other, that we need each other. He calls for a culture of encounter in which we meet each other in dignity, adamant that no human being is superfluous or useless.

He calls for a new economics that sustains, protects and regenerates, that places a higher value on the dignity of labour and a higher value on work that generates value for society, not just wealth for shareholders. He calls for the regeneration of the natural world "by living more sustainably and more soberly while meeting the needs of those who have been harmed by or excluded from the economy until now".[26] He calls for a lifestyle that rejects consumerism and "the complacent, egotistical 'well-being' that the market sells us".[27] He calls upon us to make "the restoration of our people's dignity the central objective of the post-Covid world".[28]

Many of the recent popular movements to build a more just and sustainable world share the dream of Pope Francis. I'm thinking in particular of the #metoo movement, Black Lives Matter, the refugee crisis and the climate emergency, which came into even sharper focus with the publication of the Intergovernmental Panel on Climate Change (IPCC) report in August 2021. We may not agree with every aspect of these movements, or all of their tactics, but Vatican II reminded us that the Spirit of God is at work in all people of goodwill. As Pope Francis said in *Let us Dream*, "Wherever in the world the response is immediate, close, warm and concerned, that's where God's Spirit is present."[(29)] People will join popular movements for all sorts of reasons, but for the Christian, anywhere that people of goodwill are trying to bring about a safer, more just, more flourishing society based on the bonds of love, not domination or exploitation, then the Spirit of God is at work there.

The other human virtues – justice, courage and temperance – in many ways support the process and conclusions of prudence. An understanding of justice is what prudence is constantly refining; courage will be required to act according to the ways prompted by prudence and temperance is a "cleansing" of the heart so that we can see all the more clearly, less and less in thrall to appetite, or the unjust use of the goods of the earth.

Justice

The main type of justice we have been concerned with is what might be called *social justice*, which is the disposition, or "constant and firm will",[(30)] to give to God and our neighbours "their due".[(31)] In the case of our neighbour that means "to establish in human relationships the harmony that promotes equity with regard to persons and the common good".[(32)] As we noted in Chapter 3, it is working towards "right relations" between people and institutions which ensures a "fully human life" as defined in *Gaudium et Spes*. To discern what is just and not just is the work of prudence; our calling is to be committed to social justice, to the restoration and transformation of social relationships distorted by greed and power. However, justice on its own is not enough, it must be completed by love, otherwise it's just a materialistic exercise. The other types of justice – *commutative, legal and distributive* – are covered in detail in the *Catechism* and the *Compendium of the Social Doctrine of the Church*.

Courage

Courage, or fortitude as it's sometimes known, is the virtue that ensures that we persevere in our pursuit of the common good. As we saw in the Gospels, as we've seen throughout Christian history, anybody who promotes social justice based on the dignity of the person with a preferential option for the poor, will make enemies, will be persecuted. That is perhaps not as vivid in Britain as it is in other countries where being a Christian and speaking out for the rights of the poor against the government or powerful corporations can mean risking your life. The virtue of courage, supported by grace, is the disposition of a brave heart to carry on in the face of opposition, or our own temptations to give up. It is the courage to offer ourselves up in service to others. We know the Lord is on our side, as the Psalmist said, "The Lord is my strength and my might" (Psalm 118:14). At the end of John's Gospel, Jesus says to his disciples, "Take courage; I have conquered the world" (John 16:33).

Temperance

You might associate temperance with not drinking alcohol, as in the temperance movements which sprang up in the nineteenth and twentieth centuries. This is certainly an aspect of temperance, which is moderating our desires and controlling our appetites. The practice of fasting features in most of the major religions for good reason. If we become driven by the pleasures of the flesh and self-indulgence, then there is less room for God. We become, in the term used by Walter Brueggemann, *depleted,* less than we were meant to be. That depletion could be caused by excessive consumption of alcohol, drugs, or food, or by sexual incontinence, all of which is to use our body as a means of personal gratification, rather than a means to love.

The Gospel does not invite us to starve ourselves, far from it, but it does warn against making physical and social satisfaction our main aim. The "bread of life" which feeds us is spiritual. We're also reminded in the *Catechism* that an aspect of temperance is "balance in the use of created goods".[33] This takes us back to one of our key themes since Chapter 1, which is our use of the goods of the earth. What is the impact of our lifestyle on the earth, our common home, on our neighbour, on our relationship with God? The virtue of temperance, which sounds old fashioned, could not be more relevant or important. We might call it the virtue of *living simply*. Can we live more simply, can we live with less, so that others might have their share of the goods of the earth? Can we resist the culture of desire, can we walk the Way of the Cross, not Madison Avenue?

Theological virtues

In a sense, we've been talking about the theological virtues – ***faith, hope and love*** – throughout this book, so just a few brief thoughts to end on. The theological virtues relate directly to God. They are the foundation of our moral life in this world. "They are infused by God into the souls of the faithful to make them capable of acting as his children…".[(34)]

I've stressed the aspect of biblical faith which is a simple trust in God. This is the gateway virtue, itself a gift of God. Faith is also understood as all that has been revealed to us and is taught by the Catholic Church. "The disciple of Christ must not only keep the faith and live on it, but also profess it, confidently bear witness to it and spread it."[(35)]

We confess our faith and follow Our Lord along the way of the Cross, a counter-cultural path of descent in solidarity with the victim and the outcast; a path which will attract the mockery and persecution of the culture of desire.

Hope is the virtue "by which we desire the Kingdom of heaven and eternal life as our happiness".[(36)] Through grace, the desires of this world, the old creation, die back and a new growth, a new desire, takes root in us. Hope is not the unwarranted optimism of the world. It is trust in the promises of Christ, not reliance on our own strength. It is the anchor of our soul.

Love is the new commandment, the eternal covenant, the reality of God revealed to us in Jesus, who loved us to the end. This is the love we are called upon to imitate. It is our participation in the priesthood of Christ by baptism, a gratuitous self-offering. It is not limited by category. It includes love of enemies. It is our vocation as human beings. Without love, we are nothing. "It is from the inner wellspring of love that the values of truth, freedom and justice are born and grow."[37]

Love is poured into our hearts by the Holy Spirit, through faith. It is the very life of God. The first effect of love is forgiveness, when our hearts are "turned over" by the plough of the Gospel. Love is sustained by doing, in the long, loving journey of a marriage, a religious vocation, in the care of a vulnerable loved one over time. Love is resourced and nourished by the daily bread of prayer in all its forms and expressions, by sacred scripture, by the liturgy of the Church, above all by the Eucharist, where we meet our loving God who wants to bring us to life.

Love needs to be discerning to know the most loving course of action. Love needs to be organised in order to fulfil its demand for justice. In the words of Cardinal Sin, the Archbishop of Manila who stood up to the Marcos dictatorship: "Strength without compassion is violence. Compassion without justice is mere sentiment. Justice without love is Marxism and... love without justice is baloney!"[38]

The culture we inhabit is not organised according to love, but rivalry, competition, performance. Our social relationships are often governed by contract, not covenant. Our relationship to the goods of the earth governed by ownership, not stewardship. The structures of sin are driven by personal greed and desire for power.

Our deepest identity is to live in communion with God and in loving relation with our brothers and sisters. The Church in all its manifestations should be a catalyst for transforming social structures, radically transforming relationships, building structures of solidarity in the local community, not just the parish.

The prophet Jeremiah wrote to the exiles in Babylon, the ones who sang the hymn of creation in Genesis chapter 1. He said to them, "Seek the welfare of the city where I have sent you into exile, and pray to the Lord on its behalf, for in its welfare you will find your welfare" (Jeremiah 29:7).

Church communities should be places of communion, witness and mission. Places where the needs of the community are known, where relationships are just, where voices are heard, where forgiveness is known, where our common priesthood is respected and resourced.

The disciple of Jesus Christ is formed and grows in community, is accountable to that community, and that community is accountable to them for their formation and accompaniment, for the development of their gifts.

The great pattern of the Christian life is gift followed by gratitude, proclamation followed by response. Why did God make you? Why did God make the world and send his only Son into the world to take away its sin? Why does God send his Holy Spirit to make us holy and inspire our work for his kingdom? Because "God so loved the world" (John 3:16).

How do we respond to this love as baptised Catholics, as disciples of Christ? We respond in gratitude, in faith, in humility, by cooperating with the grace of God which is always on offer. We are "sent out" into the world, to the margins, to try to see clearly, discern a Gospel course of action, and build up a kingdom of love, peace and justice. We are called to speak truth to power, to share in the prophetic mission of Jesus.

"The dignity of the human person and the common good rank higher than the comfort of those who refuse to renounce their privileges. When these values are threatened, a prophetic voice must be raised."[39]

St Paul provides our most memorable hymns to faith, hope and love. This one from his letter to the Romans is perhaps not as popular as 1 Corinthians 13:1-13 ("If I speak in the tongues of mortals and of angels..."), but has been central to our understanding of the theological virtues:

> Therefore, since we are justified by faith, we have peace with God through our Lord Jesus Christ, through whom we have obtained access to this grace in which we stand; and we boast in our hope of sharing the glory of God. And not only that, but we also boast in our sufferings, knowing that suffering produces endurance, and endurance produces character, and character produces hope, and hope does not disappoint us, because God's love has been poured into our hearts through the Holy Spirit that has been given to us.
>
> (Romans 5:1-5)

HOW

Practical resources for growing in faith through a commitment to virtue.

Making Good Decisions: A Beginner's Guide, by Brian Grogan SJ. A guide for private and public decision-making inspired by Ignatian (Jesuit) spirituality, with examples of how major figures in the Church, including St Ignatius of Loyola and St Oscar Romero, made prudent choices inspired by faith.

Just Mission: Practical Politics for Local Churches, by Helen Cameron. A practical guide for Christian communities on how to implement social justice in a local context. The last few years have seen a resurgence of social action in Christian churches, from street pastors to debt support to food banks. This book is an invaluable guide to communities who may be embarking on the journey of social justice and how an understanding of local politics and power structures is essential in bringing about change.

To the Margins: Pope Francis and the Mission of the Church, by Andrea Riccardi. From the founder of the San 'Egidio community – an international Catholic lay organisation dedicated to peacemaking, service to the poor, prayer and evangelisation – a reflection on the call of Pope Francis to go to the margins, tracing this call back through the centuries as a constant feature of the Church.

On Aquinas, by Herbert McCabe. The Dominican Herbert McCabe was known as one of the best students of the work of St Thomas Aquinas. In this book he provides a clear account of the teaching of Aquinas on virtue, with its roots in Aristotle and the Old Testament.

Chapter EIGHT References

1. *Evangelii Gaudium* (The Joy of the Gospel), 2
2. *CCC*, 1803
3. *CCC*, 1810
4. *CCC*, 1811
5. *CCC*, 1806
6. *CCC*, 1806
7. *CCC*, 1806
8. St Pope John XXIII, *Mater et Magistra* (On Christianity and Social Progress), 236
9. Pope Francis, *Let Us Dream: The Path to a Better Future* (London: Simon and Schuster, *2020), 123*
10. *Let Us Dream, 11*
11. *Let Us Dream*, 120
12. *Let Us Dream*, 123
13. *Let Us Dream*, 123
14. Herbert McCabe, *God Still Matters* (London: Continuum, 2002), 175
15. *Let Us Dream*, 120
16. *Let Us Dream*, 120
17. Herbert McCabe, 177
18. *Let Us Dream*, 21
19. *Let Us Dream*, 52
20. *CCC*, 2423
21. *Let Us Dream*, 52
22. *Let Us Dream*, 52
23. *Let Us Dream*, 53
24. *Let Us Dream*, 53
25. *Let Us Dream*, 47
26. *Let Us Dream*, 110
27. *Let Us Dream*, 126
28. *Let Us Dream*, 133

29. *Let Us Dream*, 20
30. *CCC*, 1807
31. *CCC*, 1807
32. *CCC*, 1807
33. *CCC*, 1809
34. *CCC*, 1813
35. *CCC*, 1816
36. *CCC*, 1817
37. *Compendium of the Social Doctrine of the Church*, 205
38. Ronald Rolheiser, *Seeking Spirituality: Guidelines for a Christian Spirituality of the Twenty-First Century* (London: Hodder and Stoughton, 1998), 158
39. *Evangelii Gaudium*, 39

"A heart which sees..." the Good Samaritan

What do you do when you see as God sees? A parable which might help us here is the Good Samaritan in Luke's Gospel. It might be worth having a slow read through the text before going any further (Luke 10:25-37). The parable begins when a lawyer stands up "to test Jesus" (Luke 10:25). Students of rabbis stood before their sitting teacher out of respect, but they did not "test" their teacher. The lawyer is taking the devil's role, for it was Satan who "tested" Jesus in the wilderness. So we know that this is coming from a dangerous place and is a challenge to the will of God. His question is, "Teacher, what must I do to inherit eternal life?" (10:25). Two words dominate the exchange which follows, two words which are key to the life of discipleship: "do" and "life". However, as the Jewish scripture scholar Amy-Jill Levine has pointed out, the words are used very differently by the lawyer and Jesus. The lawyer's use of the word "do" is in a grammatical tense "that suggests a single, limited action".(1) He's looking for something to tick off his salvation check-list. It's all about him and his desire to "inherit" eternal life, something he might achieve if he did the right thing.

Jesus is nimble in these situations. He's never pinned down by a "test" question. He doesn't answer the question, but he looks into the heart of the questioner: "What is written in the law? What do you read there?" (10:26). This isn't just a memory test. A lot of translations use "how" rather than "what" for the second question: *How* do you read the law? Jesus is asking for his interpretation. The lawyer answers that the law is all about love of God (Deuteronomy 6:5) and love of neighbour (Leviticus 19:18), which shows at least that he's been paying attention to Jesus. But the question he asked shows that he doesn't understand that the heart and soul of this is about a way of life, not just box-ticking. Jesus makes the point by re-framing his question. He compliments him on the apparent correctness of his answer and then says, "do this, and you will live" (10:28). Levine points out that the imperative "do" used by Jesus is not about a single action, but an ongoing relationship. Jesus also says and you "will live" as in "live now". It is not about an action that will achieve some reward in the afterlife, but living according to life-giving covenant now.

We know that the lawyer does not have good intentions, so he is not going to just humbly accept this wisdom and be on his way. He wants to "justify himself" (10:29), to make sure he enjoys approval, so he asks the leading question, "who is my neighbour?" (10:29). Levine comments that this question is a polite way of asking, "Who is *not* my neighbour?"[2] You can only define a category over against those who are not in the category. Jesus again sidesteps the question. He refuses to deal in categories, to define who is "in" and who is "out" of our neighbourly regard. Jesus has come to offer a startlingly richer and bigger vision. He doesn't issue a decree about this, or add another statute to the law. He tells a story.

He tells a story about a man who was going down from Jerusalem to Jericho, a journey of about seventeen miles, who fell into the hands of robbers. They strip him, beat him, and leave him for dead by the roadside. We don't know if the man was a Jew or not, but that is the usual assumption since if he wasn't, that would have been pointed out. His condition after he's been beaten up, however, is more primordial. He has been stripped of all the usual identity markers: no clothes, no speech, no accent. He's just an injured, naked, human being.

This whole short scene is an illustration of the human condition outside of the Garden of Eden: greed, desperation, violence, winners and losers; a victim left for dead on the road while the nameless predators fade back into the shadows, a little bit richer.

Now "by chance" (10:31) a priest comes along. That little phrase "by chance" is full of significance. What is unfolding before us are the possibilities of "doing" that come our way in the random narrative of life. This isn't planned. It's about what you come across as you're on the road and what you do next. The priest "saw him" (10:31), but what did he see? He couldn't be sure if this was a "neighbour" or not and therefore worthy of his love. In the Old Testament, neighbour was defined as "the sons of your own people" (Leviticus 19:18) and, since Israel had a memory of being strangers in a strange land, resident aliens in Egypt, the definition was expanded to include "The alien who resides with you" (Leviticus 19:34). There is a strong assumption in many Christian interpretations that the priest's aversion to the corpse-like victim is also to do with purity codes and not wanting to be defiled. Levine is unconvinced by this. The priest is coming "down" from Jerusalem to Jericho, so he's finished with his duties in the Temple; ritual defilement is not an issue. Jesus does not make any reference to ritual purity.

More to the point, saving a life was so important that "the Jewish law mandates that it override every other concern, including keeping the Sabbath".[3] The priest and the Levite who comes along after him have failed this man. Levine says that the best explanation she's heard for their refusal to help comes from Martin Luther King Jr, who preached on the Good Samaritan at a rally in support of striking sanitation workers on the eve of his assassination in Memphis, Tennessee in April 1968: "I'm going to tell you what my imagination tells me. It's possible that these men were afraid... And so the first question that the priest and the Levite asked was, 'If I stop to help this man, what will happen to me?' But then the Good Samaritan came by, and he reversed the question: 'If I do not stop to help this man, what will happen to him?' If I do not help the sanitation workers, what will happen to them?"[4]

We've been introduced to the priest and the Levite. The listeners of Jesus, attuned to folkloric patterns, would have anticipated the appearance of a third figure. This survives to this day in stories and jokes, such as "An Englishman, an Irishman and a Scotsman walk into a pub...". If a Jewish audience had heard a story beginning with a priest and a Levite they would be expecting the third figure to be "an Israelite" (Ezra 10:5; Nehemiah 11:3). But this is a Jesus parable and the unexpected is never far away. Jesus' listeners, expecting the Israelite to come along and do the right thing, would have been stunned that the third figure was a Samaritan, an enemy of the Jews and in no sense a neighbour: not one of our own, not a resident alien, but an enemy. The structure of the story changes at this point. From the sparse details of the robbery and the passing by, now we get the lavish detail of the Samaritan's attention to the victim. It starts when, unlike the first two, he "came near him" (10:33) and, in a key phrase, "was moved with pity" (10:33). Luke has already used the word "pity" (or compassion in many translations) to describe the reaction of Jesus to seeing the widow of Nain at her only son's funeral procession (7:13). Later on in the Gospel, Luke will use the same word to describe the reaction of the father to the return of his prodigal son (15:20).

William Barclay describes the Greek word used in the New Testament for pity or compassion as a "revolution in the realm of thought".[5] *Spagchnizestai* means to be moved with compassion in a deep, visceral way. Barclay describes this as the strongest word in Greek for feelings of compassion, coming from the "nobler viscera" – the heart, lungs, liver and intestines – the deepest seat of emotions for Greeks. To a Greek audience, to whom Luke's Gospel was addressed, the notion that this word was used to describe a divine attribute was incredible. Barclay comments that, "according to the Stoics, and they were the highest thinkers of the age, the supreme and essential characteristic of God is *apatheia*".[6] This apatheia did not mean apathy as we understand it, but rather being incapable of feeling. The Stoics argued that if you feel sorrow or joy it means someone else can bring this about in you and therefore has, for that moment at least, power over you, is greater than you. If God could feel pity for anything that happens to human beings it would mean that we can affect God, that we have power over him, which is impossible, since no one can be greater than God, therefore God can have no feeling. To the Stoic philosophers, the idea of a divine being moved by compassion was beyond comprehension. Yet that is exactly the picture we have in Luke's Gospel, summed up in that one word, "compassion".

In the Gospels, Jesus is moved with pity by the spiritual poverty of the crowd (Matthew 9:36; Mark 6:34). He is not angry with them, or condemning. He wants to find them, teach them, and bring them home. Jesus is moved with pity by hunger and pain. When he meets the blind men (Matthew 20:34), or the leper (Mark 1:41), he takes pity on them. He never reacts with indifference to human suffering. And his pity is never as if from a distance, as in "There! There! You poor things." It always issues in action to help: to touch, to teach, to heal; to restore to community. It is this compassion which races through the deepest heart of the Samaritan, which prompts him to reach out to the wounded one, even at risk to himself, to take him to an inn and involve others in his care, to commit to his well-being over time.

The parable has challenged any notion that "neighbour" could be defined in a way which permitted the exclusion of any group. The revelation of God in Jesus is a radical expansion of the concept of neighbour. In fact, the point is not, "who is my neighbour" but, as Jesus asked at the end of the story, "Which of these three, do you think, was a neighbour to the man?" (10:36). The subdued lawyer cannot bring himself to say the word Samaritan, but rather, "the one who showed him mercy" (10:37). Jesus then says, "Go and do likewise" (10:37). Here are the key words of Christian life – "go" and "do". What they mean in our day, in our circumstances, is what we are invited to discern. How can we be a neighbour, how can we bring the compassion of God to the wounded ones of our day? Is it just enough to bandage wounds, or should we be working to ensure that the highway from Jerusalem to Jericho is safe and well-lit?

Pope Francis says that the parable of the Good Samaritan faces us with "the basic decision we need to make in order to rebuild our wounded world".[7] In the face of so much suffering, the impact of the pandemic, the suffering that was present before the pandemic, if we do not imitate the Good Samaritan, then we are either one of the robbers or one of those who passed by. Pope Francis has consistently called upon us to examine our own lifestyles and, like the parables themselves, challenges us to ask if what we thought was a good and moral life is in fact supportive of an unjust status quo. He says there is an interplay between "those who manipulate and cheat society"[8] and those who – and this, to our discomfort, might include us – "while claiming to be detached and impartial critics, live off that system and its benefits",[9] who are, in other words, implicated in the "structures of sin" we looked at in Chapter 3. Nor can we take refuge in the complaint that any contribution I might make to a better world is a drop in the ocean. Being fully human calls us to think and act otherwise, since "we are created for a fulfilment that can only be found in love".[10] The followers of Jesus cannot be indifferent to suffering. The opposite of indifference is compassion. We are challenged to emerge from behind our walls of self-protection and "be changed by our contact with human suffering".[11]

In this parable, Jesus turns our attention away from tribal categories which circumscribe our charity and invites us to be a neighbour to all, especially the vulnerable one, to traverse all our cultural boundaries and operate out of a vision of universal fraternity, to see the world with the compassionate eyes of God. For Pope Benedict XVI this was key to the Christian life: "The Christian's programme – the programme of the Good Samaritan, the programme of Jesus – is a 'heart which sees'. This heart sees where love is needed and acts accordingly".[12] In an even more radical revelation, the victim becomes synonymous with God. In Matthew 25:31-46, in the Judgement of the Nations, the king said that in as much as you clothed the naked and gave food to the hungry, "you did it to me" (25:40).

When Jesus asked the lawyer "how" he read the law, it was because he had options. As Amy-Jill Levine tells us, "In Hebrew the words 'neighbour' and 'evil' share the same consonants (*resh ayin*); they differ only in their vowels – but ancient Hebrew texts do not have vowels."[13] So Jesus is saying to the lawyer that in the very letters of the law, neighbour and enemy are equated and so the commandment is to love both, or rather to see only one thing. The Hebrew language itself contained a kind of adumbration of the universal truth which Jesus reveals: there are no enemies, no-one undeserving of our love. We are called to inhabit the world as images of God, in a community of love, which means seeing the world and all our brothers and sisters with the eyes of compassion, with a heart which responds to suffering, with a will to build a society worthy of God.

REFLECTION References

1. Amy-Jill Levine, *Short Stories by Jesus: The Enigmatic Parables of a Controversial Rabbi* (New York: HarperOne, 2015), 84
2. Amy-Jill Levine, 93
3. Amy-Jill Levine, 102
4. Amy-Jill Levine, 102
5. William Barclay, *New Testament Words* (Louisville: Westminster John Knox Press, 1974), 276
6. William Barclay, 278
7. Pope Francis, *Fratelli Tutti* (On Fraternity and Social Friendship), 67
8. *Fratelli Tutti*, 75
9. *Fratelli Tutti*, 75
10. *Fratelli Tutti*, 68
11. *Fratelli Tutti*, 68
12. Benedict XVI, *Deus Caritas Est* (On Christian Love), 31
13. Amy-Jill Levine, 94

Mary, undoer of knots

The final chapter of *Lumen Gentium* is dedicated to the role of Mary in the Church and in salvation history. In her body, and by her willing consent, Mary received the Word made flesh into this world. The same Spirit that hovered over the waters of chaos in the beginning, hovered over Mary and conceived within her the new creation, the new Adam, the Messiah, whom she named *Yeshua*, meaning "to deliver, to rescue". The Vatican II document reminds us of the teaching of St Irenaeus, one of the early Church fathers, who saw a parallel between Eve and Mary: "The knot of Eve's disobedience was untied through the obedience of Mary; what the virgin Eve bound up through her lack of faith, the virgin Mary untied by her faith".(1) This may seem hard on Eve, perpetuating the myth that Eve, that all women, were somehow responsible for humanity's fall from grace. It has certainly been used that way over time, but there is just as much emphasis through the ages on Jesus as the second Adam, who has come into the world to get right what Adam got wrong.

This is the origin of the devotion to Mary, undoer of knots, the one who can disentangle us from the knots of worldly wisdom, the wisdom of the serpent. There is a painting of Mary, undoer of knots, by Johann Georg Melchior Schmidtner, from around 1700, which hangs in the church of St Peter am Perlach in Augsburg, Germany. When Pope Francis was studying there many years ago, he was taken by this devotion and brought a postcard of the painting back with him to Argentina. It would seem to be a suitable devotion for us as we discern the mission of the Church amidst the "knots" of a society shaken by a once in a generation pandemic. In the early Church, in the days before Pentecost, which might feel like the days we are living through today, waiting for the Spirit to regenerate and renew the Church, the disciples were in the upper room in Jerusalem, "constantly devoting themselves to prayer" (Acts 1:14), waiting for the Spirit. With them in that upper room, and with us in the upper room of our discernment, is Mary, whom the Church honours with the title "Mother of God". Mary is also invoked by the titles of "advocate, benefactress, helper and mediatrix".(2)

Mary is described by St Ambrose as the "type of the Church",(3) that is to say, "in the order of faith, charity and perfect union with Christ".(4) Mary's faith, which along with the faith of Joseph, her spouse, would have formed Jesus in the long years of his "hidden" life in the small agrarian village of Nazareth eighty miles to the north of Jerusalem, far from the religious and political centre. Mary's faith finds its fullest voice in the Magnificat, her song of praise when she visited her cousin Elizabeth, who was also pregnant. Mary's song is rooted in the Old Testament and the promises of God for his people. The "lowliness" (Luke 1:48) of Mary is the type for the disciple, a humble one who is raised up by God. She sings that God "has shown strength with his arm" (1:51). This is a new exodus, when again the Lord will be attentive to the cries of the suffering ones. The rich are "sent away empty" (1:53), they are full enough already, they have no room for God. It is the lowly who are "lifted up" (1:52). This is the good news to the poor which Jesus proclaimed around thirty years later, in the small synagogue in Nazareth, to the rage of his listeners, who were more interested in vengeance and gaining land for themselves.

Pope Francis has given new energy to popular piety, as well as giving new energy to a radical critique of the Church and society. The Church needs to draw upon all its resources in these times of challenge and renewal. The Church needs its lay people to be engaged and involved, to contribute all their gifts and enthusiasm to a reanimated mission in a post-Covid society. In the face of the frustrations of being in the Church, with so many of its flaws now laid bare, it is tempting to walk away, like the two disciples on the road to Emmaus. But we are always invited to the table where we are fed with the word and body of Christ, where sad hearts are kindled again, and we set off to rejoin the community, with Mary at its heart. This is where the disciple grows, where hearts are formed. The Church, for all its flaws, is a place of nurture, a wise mother who can keep us on the path of grace and truth.

Mary, undoer
of knots,

pray for us
entangled

in the injustice
of this world,

the schemes
of the mighty,

the seduction
of princes:

you who brought
into this world

the Lord
of the lowly.

MARY, UNDOER OF KNOTS References

1. Second Vatican Council, *Lumen Gentium*, 56
2. *Lumen Gentium*, 62
3. *Lumen Gentium*, 63
4. *Lumen Gentium*, 63